ROUTLEDGE LIBRARY EDITIONS:
MARXISM

Volume 20

MARX'S *GRUNDRISSE* AND HEGEL'S *LOGIC*

MARX'S *GRUNDRISSE* AND HEGEL'S *LOGIC*

HIROSHI UCHIDA

Edited by
TERRELL CARVER

Routledge
Taylor & Francis Group
LONDON AND NEW YORK

First published in 1988

This edition first published in 2015
by Routledge
2 Park Square, Milton Park, Abingdon, Oxon OX14 4RN

and by Routledge
711 Third Avenue, New York, NY 10017

Routledge is an imprint of the Taylor & Francis Group, an informa business

British Library Cataloguing in Publication Data
A catalogue record for this book is available from the British Library

ISBN: 978-1-138-85502-1 (Set)
ISBN: 978-1-315-71284-0 (Set) (ebk)
ISBN: 978-1-138-88850-0 (Volume 20) (hbk)
ISBN: 978-1-138-88853-1 (Volume 20) (pbk)
ISBN: 978-1-315-71338-0 (Volume 20) (ebk)

Publisher's Note
The publisher has gone to great lengths to ensure the quality of this reprint but points out that some imperfections in the original copies may be apparent.

Disclaimer
The publisher has made every effort to trace copyright holders and would welcome correspondence from those they have been unable to trace.

MARX'S *GRUNDRISSE*

AND HEGEL'S *LOGIC*

HIROSHI UCHIDA

Edited by Terrell Carver

ROUTLEDGE
London and New York

First published in 1988 by
Routledge
11 New Fetter Lane, London EC4P 4EE
29 West 35th Street, New York, NY 10001

Printed and bound in Great Britain by
Biddles Ltd, Guildford and King's Lynn
Typeset by Pat and Anne Murphy, Highcliffe-on-Sea, Dorset

British Library Cataloguing in Publication Data

Uchida, Hiroshi
Marx's Grundrisse and Hegel's Logic.
1. Society. Theories of Karl Marx, 1818–1883.
Influence of German philosophy. Hegel,
Georg Wilhelm Friedreich, 1770–1831
I. Title II. Carver, Terrell, *1946*–
301'.092'4

ISBN 0-415-00385-7

Library of Congress Cataloging-in-Publication Data

ISBN 0-415-00385-7

Contents

To the memory of
My Father, Sokichi Uchida (1902–62)
and
My Mother, Moto Uchida (1904–76)

Acknowledgements

I should like to thank Yuhikaku Publishers, Tokyo, especially Mr Shinsuke Ito, for granting permission for an English translation of my previously published work in Japanese. This book is my English translation of Chapter 3 of my book *Marx's middle-period critique of political economy* (*Chuki Marx no Keizaigakuhihan*) (Tokyo: Yuhikaku, 1985), pp. 125–78, altered and enlarged, though the arguments, quotations and references are substantially the same. I have also included part of Chapter 1 of my book, and some sections from my article 'Definitions of "Substance" in the *Grundrisse*' ('Keizaigakuhihanyoko niokeru Jittaikitei') in *Monthly Report of the Institute for Social Sciences of Senshu University* (Tokyo), 266 (20 September 1985), pp. 2–13. The Appendix, Select Bibliography and Index are new.

I am very grateful to Dr Terrell Carver, the editor of this book, for improving and polishing my clumsy English to make it readable and concise. If this book has something to contribute to the international academic study of Karl Marx, I owe most to him for that merit. Needless to say, I am entirely responsible for any mistakes and defects.

My work on this book was accomplished between January and April 1987 in my study room at the Department of Politics, University of Bristol, where I have been Visiting Professor for the academic year 1986–7. I am greatly indebted to Professor J. M. Lee, Head of the Politics Department, for arranging this stay, to others on the academic staff, and to the secretaries — Mrs Mary Woods, for her high sense of humour, and Miss Anne Dempsey, for her thoughtfulness and understanding. I am especially grateful to Dr George Sanford for kindly introducing me to the publishers Routledge.

I have been greatly impressed with the high quality of service provided by the staff of the University Library at Bristol. I shall remember them always with gratitude for their help.

My accommodation for the year has been at Burwalls, the Short-Course and Conference Centre of the Univeristy of Bristol. How often I have enjoyed the commandingly beautiful view of Bristol at night from the window of my room, and how it made me think of my family in Japan! I am very grateful to Mr Derek Smith and the other staff at Burwalls for their splendid hospitality.

It is my pleasure to express gratitude to Senshu University, Tokyo, particularly to my colleagues at the Department of Economics, for giving me this fruitful year for academic study.

Last but not least, I am very grateful to Mr Andrew Lockett, Editor for Social Sciences at Routledge, who has encouraged me to publish this book.

Hiroshi Uchida
Bristol

Editor's Introduction

It has been my very great pleasure to assist Hiroshi Uchida in preparing his own translation of his Japanese book and other materials for the press, and to have had the benefit of his company during his year at the University of Bristol. His work is of major significance for contemporary scholarship on Karl Marx, and I warmly recommend it to an English readership.

Marx's *Grundrisse* manuscripts, unpublished until 1939–41 and virtually unknown in the West until the 1960s, have been the object of increasing scholarly attention, translation and commentary. Since the mid-1970s, when an English version became readily available, interest has steadily quickened. The relation of Marx's work as a whole to that of the philosopher G. W. F. Hegel has been an important issue in interpreting Marx since 1859, when Friedrich Engels first declared it to be crucial. This is a point reiterated by V. I. Lenin and numerous more academic commentators.

Professor Uchida's book is the first full-length study that links Marx's *Grundrisse* to Hegel's *Logic* in a thorough textual analysis that makes the connections explicit. Moreover this book is also the first work to appear in English that reflects a lively tradition of Japanese scholarship and debate about the nature and implications of Marx's thought. Books by Japanese economists on Marx have been available in English translation for some time, but more wide-ranging textual, methodological and philosophical inquiries have not, till now, reached a western audience.

Marx's 'Grundrisse' and Hegel's 'Logic' is a complex but rewarding work. The *Grundrisse* is acknowledged as a vital text linking Marx's early works, especially the *Economic and philosophical manuscripts (1844)*, which revolutionised western thought about Marx in the 1960s, to his later work in the volumes of *Capital*, works revered by Marxists but not as widely read outside Marxist circles, or even within them, as other classic texts by Marx, or Engels.

For some western commentators the 'Hegelian' character of the *Grundrisse* revealed a continuity between the early and late Marx that undermined the prevailing view that he had cast aside philosophy in favour of the science manifested in his work on history, bourgeois society and materialist dialectics. For other writers the

Grundrisse was an important key to Marx's work in *Capital* on the capitalist economy, its historical origin and progress, and the general structure and processes of human social development. In particular the *Grundrisse* provided some illumination of the mysterious passages in the prefaces to *Capital* in which Marx, on his own admission, 'coquetted' with Hegelian terminology. Perhaps startlingly for someone who advertised his own work as scientific, empirical and methodologically comparable in certain respects to the natural sciences, Marx openly avowed himself a pupil of Hegel, 'that mighty thinker'.

Those facts raise a number of puzzles, and Uchida's book provides a wealth of material to help us formulate answers. Very broadly, the relationship between science and philosophy is at stake. To what extent are science and philosophy unrelated or even opposing modes of thought? If they are related and perhaps compatible, how exactly is this so? More specifically, what is Marx's special contribution to that debate? What exactly do his criticisms of Hegel offer us in terms of insights, methods, results?

Those questions cannot be addressed without looking carefully at Hegel's work. Its originality and even uniqueness are not in question, but it rests on a wide-ranging synthesis of many other writers, tempered with critical re-interpretation. Most notable among these authors, for our purposes, are Aristotle and Adam Smith. Uchida has delved into these matters of textual scholarship much more thoroughly than any previous commentator, noting that Marx made direct use of Aristotle and Smith, as did Hegel. Consequently in Marx's works we are reading a complex dialogue with and around Hegel that takes in classical philosophy and classical political economy.

None of the classic writers I have mentioned would have considered it surprising to link philosophy and logic, on the one hand, with history and economics on the other, and it is not very much to our credit that since Marx's time these subjects have drifted so far apart that the very idea of reuniting them in order to pose and answer common questions is hardly thinkable. Because of this drift, the very questions concerning contemporary society that Marx wanted to ask, and the techniques that he used to state and answer them, have become difficult for us to understand, and we are not at all well off in this position.

Uchida argues that Marx's critique of political economy — yielding his social science of capitalism — and Marx's critique of Hegel — yielding new 'materialist' presuppositions and a 'dialectical' method — are doubly interrelated. Firstly, Marx adapted Hegelian logic in order to analyse the economic categories crucial to modern society. But secondly, Hegel's logical categories were themselves reflections of the productive processes, even the economic categories, of contemporary commercial society. Thus Marx's critique of the political economists is simultaneously a critique of Hegel and other idealist philosophers, and his critique of Hegel and idealism is simultaneously a critique of political economy and contemporary commercial practice.

Uchida reveals a conceptual structure common to the apparently rarefied world of Hegelian conceptual logic and to the supposedly commonsensical world of economic science. Demonstrating this is a considerable achievement, and it allows us to consider precisely what is valuable today in Marx's critical commentary on this conceptual structure and on the type of society in which it is manifested. Uchida's subject, like Marx's, is 'the force of capital on modern life'.

Marx's 'Grundrisse' and Hegel's 'Logic' is textual in method and dramatic in its implications. I warmly recommend it to the English-speaking world.

Terrell Carver
University of Bristol

Abbreviations

Full references for the works cited below are in the Select Bibliography.

Capital:
Karl Marx, *Capital*, vol. 1, trans. Ben Fowkes; vols 2 and 3, trans. David Fernbach.

Z:
G. W. F. Hegel, *Logic*, trans. W. Wallace. Quotations from this 'Minor logic' are cited by section number and, where necessary, 'Z' (for *Zusatz* or Supplement). Quotations from this translation have sometimes been altered with reference to the German text in *Enzyklopädie der Philosophischen Wissenschaften*.

N:
Karl Marx, *Grundrisse*, trans. M. Nicolaus. Quotations from this translation have sometimes been altered with reference to the German text in *Ökonomische Manuskripte 1857/58*. Substantive insertions into the text are identified by '— HU'; other insertions in brackets are in the original text, except where I have inserted German terms, which have been modernised in spelling. (Extracts reproduced by permission of Penguin Books Ltd, translation copyright © Martin Nicolaus, 1973.)

M:
Karl Marx, *Ökonomische Manuskripte 1857/58*.

Manuscripts (1844):
Karl Marx, *Economic and philosophical manuscripts (1844)*, trans. Gregor Benton.

Phenomenology of spirit:
G. W. F. Hegel, *Phenomenology of spirit*, trans. A. V. Miller.

Science of logic:
G. W. F. Hegel's *Science of logic*, trans. A. V. Miller. Quotations from this text have been compared with the translation by Johnston and Struthers and with the German text in *Wissenschaft der Logik*.

Werke:
Marx–Engels Werke, vols 29–31.

Preface

This book[1] deals with the relation between Karl Marx's *Grundrisse* and the *Logic* of G. W. F. Hegel.[2] I attempt to prove that the relation is more profound and more systematic than hitherto appreciated.

Marx's application of Hegel's *Logic* to the *Grundrisse* was first mentioned in a letter, written around 16 January 1858, to Friedrich Engels:

> In my *method* of working [*Methode des Bearbeitens*] it has given me great service that by mere accident I had again leafed through Hegel's *Logic* — Freiligrath found some volumes of Hegel which originally belonged to Bakunin and sent me them as a present.[3]

Many students of Marx have referred to the letter and have discussed it, but Marx's use of Hegel's *Logic* in the *Grundrisse* has not been fully examined. Let us consider some representative writers who have concerned themselves with the relationship.

There are the editors of the original German edition of the *Grundrisse* (*Grundrisse der Kritik der Politischen Ökonomie (Rohentwurf)*, Dietz Verlag, Berlin, 1953). This photocopy edition of the original two volumes of 1939 and 1941 has end-notes, many of which refer to Hegel's *Logic*. A reader using these notes, however, inevitably fails to find the hidden use of Hegel's *Logic* in the *Grundrisse*, because the notes are not based on a correct understanding of Marx's critique. These notes only create confusion.

Roman Rosdolsky wrote *The making of Marx's 'Capital'*, the pioneering study of the *Grundrisse*, whilst 'inhabiting a city whose libraries contained only very few German, Russian or French socialist works', and so he was able to use only 'the few books in his own possession'.[4] He nevertheless became aware of the relation of Hegel's *Logic* to Marx's *Grundrisse*, and wrote:

> The more the work advanced, the clearer it became that I would only be able to touch upon the most important and theoretically interesting problem presented by the 'Rough Draft' — that of the relation of Marx's work to Hegel, in

> particular to the *Logic* — and would not be able to deal with it in any greater depth.[5]

Although he thought that he could only 'touch upon' the problem, and that he could not 'deal with it in any greater depth', he ventured to remark:

> If Hegel's influence on Marx's *Capital* can be seen explicitly only in a few footnotes, the 'Rough Draft' must be designated as a massive reference to Hegel, in particular to his *Logic* — irrespective of how radically and materialistically Hegel was inverted! The publication of the *Grundrisse* means that the academic critics of Marx will no longer be able to write without first having studied his method and its relation to Hegel.[6]

The fact that Hegel's influence on Marx's *Capital* is largely implicit was suggested in Marx's letter of 9 December 1861 to Engels: '. . . the thing [*Critique of political economy 1861–3*] is assuming a much more popular form, and the method is much less in evidence than in Part I' [i.e. *A contribution to the critique of political economy* of 1859].[7] This letter relates to the manuscripts of 1861–3, but the case is the same with *Capital*. Compared with *Capital* (or the manuscripts of 1861–3), the *Grundrisse* has many explicit references to Hegel, to the *Logic*. Rosdolsky, who studied with 'a number of difficulties', suggested that Marx critically utilised Hegel's *Logic* in writing the *Grundrisse*. However, Rosdolsky did not fulfil the task of proving this in his book.

Rosdolsky referred eight times to Hegel in his study of the 'Chapter on Money' from the *Grundrisse*, and nine times when he considered the 'Chapter on Capital'.[8] He indicated a few specific points where Marx's critique of political economy was carried out in reference to the *Logic*. Most of the examples which Rosdolsky gave his readers are arbitrary and not relevant to the theoretical context of the *Grundrisse*. This should be said, albeit in the light of the difficulties which he endured whilst writing his study of the *Grundrisse*, the first variant of *Capital*.

Martin Nicolaus, the English translator of the *Grundrisse* in the Pelican Marx Library, has a similarly high opinion of the importance of Hegel's *Logic* in the 'Rough Draft'. In the Foreword to the English translation of the *Grundrisse* Nicolaus wrote as follows:

> If one considers not only the extensive use of Hegelian

> terminology in the *Grundrisse*, not only the many passages which reflect self-consciously on Hegel's method and the use of the method, but also the basic structure of the argument in the *Grundrisse*, it becomes evident that the services rendered Marx by his study of the *Logic* were very great indeed.[9]

Readers of Nicolaus's introductory Foreword[10] naturally expect him to refer to the crucial points where the *Grundrisse* contains a critical application of the *Logic*. However, this expectation is not fulfilled, though the *Grundrisse* contains several footnotes to the *Logic*.[11] Those footnotes are never sufficient to explain how the *Logic* was critically absorbed as a whole and in detail in the *Grundrisse*. For example, though Nicolaus properly noted that Marx relates 'production' to Hegel's 'ground' (*Grund*),[12] he failed to recognise that the reference is intimately connected with Marx's conception of money in its third determination as 'a contradiction which dissolves itself'.[13] The same expression appears just before 'ground' in the *Logic*.

Nor did Nicolaus notice that Marx refers 'means of production' to 'matter' (*Materie*) and 'labour-power' to 'form' (*Form*) in the *Logic*, and he mistranslated the German term *Materie* as 'material'.[14] Therefore it may be helpful to remind readers of the Nicolaus translation that they should consult the original German text if they wish to rediscover Hegel's *Logic* in the *Grundrisse*.[15]

Besides Hegel, Aristotle should be considered in connection with philosophical aspects of the *Grundrisse*. Alfred Schmidt commented on this in his excellent work, *The concept of nature in Marx*: 'Although the *Grundrisse* contains an extraordinary amount of new material on the question of Marx's relation to Hegel and, through Hegel, to Aristotle, they have so far hardly been used in discussions of Marx's philosophy.'[16] Marx's comments in his letter of 21 December 1857 to Ferdinand Lassalle are evidence that he was most interested in Aristotle whilst writing the *Grundrisse*: 'I always had great interest in the latter philosopher [Heraclitus], to whom I prefer only Aristotle of the ancient philosophers.'[17]

Schmidt is correct to point out the use of Aristotle in the 'Rough Draft', remarking that Marx approached Aristotle through Hegel. However, Schmidt failed to find any direct use of Aristotle by Marx. As we will see later, Marx does refer directly to him, for instance, when he posits the commodity at the beginning of the 'Chapter on Money' as the concrete instantiation (*synolon*) of the primary substance (*prōtē ousia*) and the secondary substance (*deuterai ousiai*).[18]

However, Schmidt made a noteworthy suggestion concerning the use of Aristotle in the *Grundrisse*:

> Here [in the *Grundrisse*] Marx tried to grasp the relation of Subject and Object in labour by using pairs of concepts, such as 'form–matter', or 'reality–possibility', which stem from Aristotle, whom he rated highly as a philosopher. In an immediate sense, of course, Marx depended on the corresponding categories of Hegel's logic, but as they are interpreted materialistically their Aristotelian origin shines more clearly through than it does in Hegel himself.[19]

According to Schmidt, Marx used Aristotle to construct a materialist basis for his theory, and he used Hegel to inquire why and how modern life is alienated and appears in an idealist form. Hegel, though thinking himself to be the greatest Aristotelian, actually deformed Aristotle's philosophy. He changed what Aristotle defined as 'active reason', which existed in every individual, into 'substance as subject'.[20]

In my view, Marx attempts to reform Hegel's philosophy using materialist aspects of Aristotle's philosophy, in order to prove why and how modern life is developed through the force of capital. His critique of Hegel does not simply reduce his idealism to a materialist basis, but consists in converting his philosophy of alienation (*Entfremdung*) and reification (*Versachlichung*) into historical categories. He uses these to clarify perverted life in capitalism, and he reads Hegel's 'idea' as a form of bourgeois consciousness.

Marx's use of Hegel's *Logic* in the formation of *Capital* can be summarised as follows:

1. In the *Economic and philosophical manuscripts (1844)* he studies not only the *Phenomenology of spirit* and the *Philosophy of right*, but also the *Encyclopaedia*. He characterises the 'Minor Logic' as 'the money of the spirit'. This means that the *Logic* is the most abstract philosophical expression of the bourgeois spirit or consciousness of value. This consciousness of value forms the basic economic relation of bourgeois society.[21]

2. In *The holy family* of 1845 he discusses Hegel's mode of presentation, writing, for example, that many forms of fruit really exist, so 'man' may abstract 'fruit in general' as an idea. Hegel, however, reverses the process, insisting that at the beginning 'fruit in general' exists (*ist*) as substance, and it posits many particular

forms of fruit as positive subjects. Marx reveals the secret of Hegel's philosophy, which presupposes an ideal subject *par excellence*, even though this subject is in reality a 'thought-product' or abstraction that exists merely in the mind.

3. In the *Poverty of philosophy* of 1847, Marx implies a simultaneous critique of political economy and of Hegel's philosophy, especially the *Logic*, when he criticises Pierre-Joseph Proudhon's *System of economic contradictions, or the philosophy of poverty* of 1846.

4. In the *Grundrisse* of 1857–8 Marx at last develops his critique of political economy and of Hegel's philosophy, especially the *Logic*, which he claims Proudhon misread. In Marx's view Proudhon grounded his socialism falsely. Marx uses a critical reading of the two classics to undermine Proudhon's theory of socialism.

5. Whilst writing the *Critique of political economy 1861–3*, Marx re-reads the 'Minor Logic' and takes notes from it.[22] Although his method of working in these manuscripts is 'much less in evidence', as already mentioned, the fact that he seems to apply the *Logic* to these manuscripts should not be overlooked.

6. As is well known, in the Postface to the second German edition of *Capital*, Marx recalls his criticism of 'the mystificatory side of the Hegelian dialectic' in *The holy family*, and announces:

> I . . . openly avowed myself the pupil of that mighty thinker, and even, here and there in the chapter on the theory of value, coquetted with the mode of expression peculiar to him. The mystification which the dialectic suffers in Hegel's hands by no means prevents him from being the first to present its general forms of motion in a comprehensive and conscious manner. With him it is standing on its head. It must be inverted, in order to discover the rational kernel within the mystical shell.[23]

Terrell Carver correctly suggested that Marx's 'rational kernel' is Hegel's analysis of logic and the 'notion', and 'the mystical shell' is Hegel's confusion of categorial movement with reality.[24] The difficulty in reading Hegel's *Logic*, however, consists in making a clear distinction between these two aspects and giving concrete examples from the text. In the text Hegel describes the process of 'becoming' (*Werden*) of the 'notion' as simultaneously the process in which the 'idea', the mystical subject, posits itself as reality. The *Grundrisse* is the first text in which Marx attempts to relate the 'becoming' of the 'subject' to the categories of political economy, and therefore there is more evidence of his analysis in it than in *Capital*, which displays his solution. The *Grundrisse* is the most suitable text for studying the relation of the critique of political economy to the *Logic*.

The correspondence of each part of the *Grundrisse* to the *Logic* is briefly summarised as follows:

1. The Introduction corresponds to the Doctrine of the Notion.
2. The 'Chapter on Money' corresponds to the Doctrine of Being.
3. The 'Chapter on Capital' corresponds to the Doctrine of Essence.

If the relation were not conceptualised this way, it would never become visible as 'an artistic whole'.[25]

The themes of the *Grundrisse* can be summarised in the following way:

For Marx, Hegel's *Logic* is 'the *money* of the spirit', the speculative '*thought-value* [*Gedankenwert*] of man and nature'.[26] This means that in bourgeois society 'man' and nature, and body and mind, are separated and reconnected through the relation of private exchange. Their relation is alienated from the persons who form the relation, which is mediated by value. They become 'value-subjects', and those who possess enough value also rule the society. The *Logic* in fact describes the value-subject abstractly.

In bourgeois society the value-subject also rules nature, the indispensable condition of life, because the subject monopolises physical as well as mental labour, so the non-possessor of nature is forced to engage in physical work. This coercion is seemingly non-violent and is legally mediated through the value-relation on which modern property is founded.[27] In modern society there is widespread acceptance of the legitimacy of one person controlling the product of another's labour, and the other's labour itself, in order to appropriate a surplus product. This approval is founded on the value-relation and the 'form' of the commodity.

Value is abstract and imagined in the mind, and also embodied in money. Hegel's *Logic* implicitly ascribes a sort of power to money, and Marx presents it as the demiurgos of bourgeois society. That is why he characterises the *Logic* as 'the money of the spirit'. His task in the *Grundrisse* therefore consists in demonstrating that the genesis of value and its development into capital are described in the *Logic*, albeit in a seemingly closed system which reproduces itself, and overall his work is directed towards transcending capitalism in practice.

1
The Introduction to the *Grundrisse* and the Doctrine of the Notion

Production in general and 'the life-process'

Marx begins the Introduction to the *Grundrisse* as follows: 'The object before us, to begin with, *material production*. Individuals producing in society — hence socially determined individual production — is, of course, the point of departure' (N 83, M 21).

In the first section of the Introduction Marx does not directly refer to Hegel by name. Rather he explicitly criticises the political economists (Adam Smith, David Ricardo etc.) for defining historically-determined individuals, material production and society in general terms. In the quotation above, however, he also implies a critique of Hegel. This is accomplished through a critique of political economy as follows:

1. The object of political economy is material production, not in general, but rather capitalist production in particular. Capital necessitates specific mental activities to mediate, maintain and increase value. Marx asks if Hegel grasps material production in that way.

2. Marx asks whether individuals are involved in material production as human beings in a general sense or in historically specific societies. Simultaneously he inquires into the historical characteristics of the metabolic system in which 'man' and nature are organised, and asks if Hegel properly addresses the problems this poses.

3. Marx asks how individuals are organised socially in order to carry out material production, and he inquires if Hegel recognises a historically specific form through which individuals relate to each other.

In the first section of Marx's Introduction to the *Grundrisse* Hegel does not seem to be relevant to the questions which are discussed. However, if the first section of the Introduction is compared with Hegel's work on 'life' under the 'idea' in the Doctrine of the Notion, it becomes evident that Marx is implicitly considering Hegel's theory of 'life' in the *Logic* in relation to the economists' theories of material production.

Hegel defines the human individual as the individual in general or the living individual:

> The first is the process of the living being *inside* itself. In that process it makes a split on its own self, and reduces its corporeity to its object or its *inorganic* nature. This corporeity, as an aggregate of correlations, enters in its very nature into difference and opposition of its elements, which mutually become each other's prey, and assimilate one another, and are retained by producing themselves. Yet this action of the several members [*Glieder*] is only the living subject's one act to which their productions revert; so that in these productions nothing is produced except the subject: in other words, the subject only reproduces itself (sect. 218).

In the above quotation human being is defined as 'living being'. The human body is separated from the human mind. The individual body is reproduced as a physical subject through the activities of its various members or organs. There is an analogy to these activities in Aristotle's 'ability to nourish'. When Hegel talks about the natural self-reproduction of human life, he treats the human body in isolation from the human mind or consciousness.

However, according to Marx the specific characteristic of human life is that it has consciousness. This appears in his *Economic and philosophical manuscripts (1844)*. He thinks that when human beings obtain food they not only ingest calories but also generate and express their culture.

Hegel, on the contrary, defines human beings as mere existence, and does not inquire into the specific mode of human life which varies regionally and historically. After that definition he discusses mental activity in a way that is indifferent to material life.

Marx sees in Hegel's account the bourgeois division of labour into physical and mental activities. In Marx's view human beings are born not only with nutritive capabilities, but with mental ones that are inseparable from them. Human beings engage in their own process of reproduction with both material and mental capabilities united as a whole. Hegel, by contrast, treats the process of reproduction as spontaneous, alien to human sensibility, needs and thought. In this view Marx finds certain characteristics of bourgeois private property.

Bourgeois private property separates physical and mental labour by means of exchange-relations based on private property, taking the superiority of mental labour over physical for granted. Human life is maintained in the metabolic process of individuals with nature. On that point Hegel writes:

> But the judgement [*Ur-Teil* = 'original division'] of the Notion proceeds, as free, to discharge the *objective* [physical] or bodily nature as an independent totality from itself; and the negative relation of the living thing to itself makes, as *immediate* individuality, the *pre-supposition* [*Voraus-Setzung* = 'the pre-posited', altered in spelling to express its objective sense] of an inorganic nature confronting it . . . The dialectic by which the object, being *implicitly* null, is merged, is the action of the self-assured living thing, which in *this process against* an *inorganic nature* thus *retains, develops*, and *objectifies* itself (sect. 219).[1]

In the quotation above Hegel defines the metabolic process of 'man' with nature. 'Man' constantly works on nature outside 'him', and obtains the means of life and enjoys them. Hegel remarks that 'man' not only maintains 'himself', but develops and objectifies 'himself'. However, this development and objectification depend on the natural unity of physical and mental activities. Hegel takes up 'man' as a merely physical existence and only later (sect. 222) does he introduce mental abilities.

It is a limitation of Hegel's work that he defines 'man' in the metabolic process as a mere physical existence. Can 'man' produce wealth without mental ability? In Hegel's conception of 'man' a specific aspect of the bourgeois economy becomes evident. This is the aspect in which the physical labourer (wage-worker) carries out material production under the command of a mental labourer (capitalist). Hegel unconsciously describes the wage-worker when he defines 'man' in the metabolic process simply as a physical existence.

Marx notes that Hegel is silent on the separation of labour into physical and mental that is characteristic of capitalism. From Marx's point of view it is a misunderstanding to accept Hegel's conception of the physical elements in 'man's' metabolism with nature as a general definition common to every form of production.

In Marx's view 'man' is born from nature with physical and mental abilities united. Marx's materialism should be understood in this way. The unity of physical and mental abilities is subsequently separated by the bourgeois value-relation.

Marx's second task is to examine Hegel's conception of the origin of society. He finds it in the sexual relation between man and woman, or in the 'genus', as follows:

> The process of *genus* [*Gattung*] brings it to *Being-for-itself* [*Fürsichsein*]. Life being no more than the immediate idea, the product of this process breaks up into two sides. *On the one side*, the living individual, which was at first presupposed [or preposited] as immediate, is now seen to be *mediated* and *generated*. *On the other*, however, the living *individuality*, which, on account of its first *immediacy*, stands in a *negative* attitude towards generality, *sinks* in the superior power of the latter (sect. 221; quotation largely altered).[2]

Hegel's discussion of 'being-for-itself' in the *Logic* argues that the individual expresses himself in relation to another, who takes the role of, so to speak, a mirror. Here (sect. 221) the individual breaks into man and woman, and they express themselves in sexual relations to bear their child, a new individual. In reality, 'being-for-itself' is the reproduction of 'man' as child through the sexual relationship between man as father and woman as mother. Parents become aged and die, so 'the living being dies' (sect. 221, Z).

However, Hegel does not ask in what form of society individuals as men and women conduct this relationship, but instead takes this association to be a purely natural or sexual one. However, men and women relate to each other in a determinate society. Through the level of development of their society it is determined how much their relationship is humanised. The specificity of society is manifested in the sexual relation as well.[3] Their relationship is not simply a physiological relation, but one in which they produce a future for their child. Although they die as individuals, they live in their child, their hope. Hegel writes: 'The death of merely immediate and individual vitality is the *emergence* [*Hervorgehen*] *of spirit*' (sect. 222).

Hegel evidently thinks that even if an individual dies, the human spirit remains. Hegel's 'idea' displays the influence of Aristotle's theory of 'active reason'.[4] The spirit which has emerged from the death of the individual and has become independent is Aristotle's 'active reason', appropriated by Hegel. However, after their deaths human beings leave various forms of spiritual wealth which continue to exist through being appreciated by the living. Hegel mistakes the appropriation of spiritual wealth by the living for a spirit independent of human beings. They leave behind not only their culture but material wealth or civilisation. Their children live with a power ruling over society, the culture and civilisation which their parents have left them.

Hegel thus defines the individual merely as a physical being, the process of metabolism as production in general, and the social relation of individuals as a merely sexual relation. He abstracts their historically specific social characteristics. Though his definitions appear naturalistic, they are in fact an abstraction of specific aspects of historical reality. The standpoint from which Hegel considers 'man' indicates that he takes it for granted that most 'men' are socially determined as a physical existence alienated from mental activity. He thinks that the separation of mental activity from physical is natural as a matter of fact and that modern private property is a manifestation of this, though these arguments are not consciously made.

In other words, in his *Logic* Hegel expresses a specific form of society as natural or universal. In that form of society physical ability (*causa efficiens*, efficient cause, *archē*) and mental ability (*causa finalis*, final cause, *eidos*), are separated and mental ability is superior to and rules over physical. If it is possible to say that as the suffix '-ism' may express some sort of state in which something is dominant, e.g. alcohol-ism or capital-ism, Hegel's 'ideal-ism' may be interpreted as a state in which the idea is dominant as a positing subject. In Hegel's idealism Marx sees the abstract reflection of modern civil society or capitalism where the ideal subject, i.e. increasing value, is dominant. This is the third point in his implicit critique.

Hegel presupposes the individual in general, abstracting from the society in which he actually lives. The very image of the independent person, e.g. the Robinson Crusoe-type, is but 'the anticipation of "civil society", in preparation since the sixteenth century and making giant strides towards maturity in the eighteenth' (N 83, M 21).

Hegel treats the metabolic process of 'man' with nature as a natural process or production in general, that is, he perversely generalises capitalist production. This is determined by the circuit of productive capital, as we will see later in Chapter 3. The definition of capital given by Adam Smith and David Ricardo, in which capital is represented as a mere condition of production, comes from such a reification (*Versachlichung*) of self-increasing value. Whereas Hegel abstracts the human being into a merely physical existence, Marx sees the capitalist division of labour and production lurking behind Hegel's abstraction.

In the 'Minor Logic' Hegel discusses 'life' (sects. 216–22) only as a physical life carried out by physical labour, then moves on to 'recognition' (sect. 223–35), which he treats as an activity of the human mind on a level quite separate from physical life. He defines mental activity only as 'recognition', and in this Marx finds a crucial problem. He acknowledges this problem but does not confine himself to mental aspects of human labour in his discussion of production in general. Rather he is concerned with mental activity in the capitalist economy.

In considering production in general Marx takes the human mind and body to be naturally united. This unity is broken by the capitalist division of labour in which the capitalist appears as mental labourer and the wage-worker as physical labourer. The capitalist orders the worker to labour in material production. Capital itself necessitates and posits a specific person, the capitalist, who mediates it. The capitalist has a mission to measure capital-value, which has to be maintained and increased in prospect during production. The capitalist's mental activity continues in the process of circulation which actualises this possibility. Capital is personified in the capitalist, who internalises its value in capitalist consciousness.

Although Hegel seems to define the process of human life as one in which 'man' engages only as a physical existence, he unconsciously reproduces capitalist production from the theoretical standpoint of the capitalist, without acknowledging this. As we will see later in detail, the 'subject' in the Doctrines of Being and of Essence is an ideal subject *par excellence*. In a certain respect Marx finds that Hegel's subject implies a specific person engaged in capitalist activity. That person appears as the spiritual subject of an organism which, so Hegel explains, eternally reproduces itself as a process of recognition. In fact Hegel's conception represents for Marx the demiurgos of bourgeois society: value and capital.

Hegel's idealism, especially in the *Logic*, expresses the capitalist mode of production abstractly, giving an account of its potential and essence. Unawares, he indicts capitalist production by defining the subject of the metabolic process as a merely physical labourer divorced from mental labour. The absence of mental labour in his definition of material life is a clue to certain features of his work. Marx explicates what Hegel has expressed only implicitly.

Critique of political economy and production in general

In the second section of the Introduction to the *Grundrisse*, Marx again undertakes a critique of Hegel in the form of a critique of political economy, even though Hegel does not appear by name. The validity of this undertaking will become apparent when we consider the third section of his Introduction.

Marx considers three pairs of concepts — consumption and production, distribution and production, and exchange and production — derived from the four categories of political economy — production, consumption, distribution and exchange. Then he clarifies the permutations between each pair of categories in order to show that they form a self-producing totality. And he demonstrates that, though the political economists seem to describe production in general, they in fact describe capitalist production from the standpoint of the circuit of productive capital (P . . . C–M–C . . . P), where the determinations of capital are invisible.

Consumption and production

Marx sets the pair in reverse order so production is last, and this is the same with the other two pairs. This order gives a clue to his critique of the political economists.

Because Adam Smith studies capital from the viewpoint of the circuit of productive capital, he believes that the movement of capital starts from production. Therefore, with respect to the relation of production to consumption, he considers individual consumption as an act apart from production, and he does not take it up in relation to production. He thinks that individual consumption is unproductive and should be restrained in order to increase capital-stock, which is to be invested as capital in production. He merely affirms consumption when it is productive, and he emphasises parsimony as a subjective fact in capitalist accumulation. Though he asserts that the purpose of production is individual consumption, in fact he theorises production for the sake of production.

However, is individual consumption always unproductive? The individual returns to the process of production afterwards, not only with physical abilities reproduced, but with some knowledge of production and a revitalised morale. The political economist omits the subjective aspect of reproduction, which is typically shown to move from consumption back to production. But why does the political economist abstract from the subjective factor? This is because production is considered from the capitalist standpoint, so in this way any funds to reproduce the lives of workers appear as costs to be reduced. The subjective factor belongs to and is monopolised by the capitalist.

Distribution and production

Here we find the same problems as above. Political economists, such as David Ricardo, bring into focus the distribution of a nett product or surplus product amongst industrial capitalists and landlords, analysing the rate of distribution of profit or surplus-value which determines the rate of capitalist accumulation. In this sense, Ricardo is an economist of distribution and capitalist accumulation.[5]

However, for Marx the most basic relation in capitalism is the one between capitalist and wage-worker, and it is between them that the conditions of production are distributed. The means of production belong to the capitalist, and labour-power to the wage-labourer. Therefore the relations of distribution include not only the distribution of surplus-value but the distribution or separation of the subjective and objective conditions of production, which is the basic presupposition of capitalism. Ricardo considers only the means of production, taking labour-power for granted as a natural presupposition. In this lacuna there lies the crucial problem of the distribution or alienation of the conditions of production in capitalism.

This distribution or separation is presupposed historically when the process of capitalist production begins and then brings about these alienated conditions as effects, so reproducing the capital relation.

The process of capitalist production is as follows:

1. distribution or separation of the conditions of production;
2. production of surplus-value;
3. distribution of surplus-value.

By contrast Ricardo's order of things is to consider production by way of the distribution of surplus-value, and to proceed back to production in this circuit of productive capital.

Exchange and production

We find the same problems here. Smith sees the process from the standpoint of the circuit of productive capital, even when he considers exchange. Marx defines three kinds of exchange:

1. immediate exchange, which links labourers within a division of labour, but without commodity-exchange;
2. commodity-exchange, which links labourers within a division of labour in commercial society (P . . . C–M–C . . . P);
3. independent exchange, which functions as an end in itself (M–C–M′).

For Marx the essential nature of exchange is manifested in the third form. The content of this kind of exchange is represented by an increase in money or value (M′–M=ΔM). This movement towards increasing value subsumes production (M–C . . . P . . . C′–M′), and moreover it turns into a movement to produce as an end in itself, i.e. the circuit of productive capital (P . . . C′–M′–M–C . . . P). It is from this standpoint that Smith observes exchange.

The third form of exchange listed above includes the process of realising surplus-value (C′–M′). From Smith's viewpoint, however, it is secondary, since to him it is a process for obtaining the conditions of production.

The nature of exchange, when it serves to increase value, is not visible to Smith, nor is it comprehensible to him that the increase of value begins with an exchange between labour-power as a commodity and money as capital, both of which are productively consumed in order to produce surplus-value in the process of capitalist production.

Because money-capital is powerful enough to link the separate conditions of production, including science and technology, the productive power of social labour appears as if it were an aspect of capital. The mental labour of the capitalist in pursuing an increase in the value of capital also appears as if it produces material wealth. Smith cannot see beneath the circuit of money-capital, which increases capital-value, because it moves within the visible circuit of productive capital. Therefore he defines money merely as a means of exchange.

Marx analyses the capitalist determinations of production, consumption, distribution and exchange as moments of capital, so what economists call 'production in general' is not trans-historical, but is in fact production based on capital, or production which includes the determinations of capital. In the lacunae in their analyses are buried the capitalist determinations of these four categories.

The nature of this omission is the same with Hegel. When he mentions 'life' (human individual), 'life-process' (the process of metabolism between man and nature) and 'species' (social relation) in which the individual is linked with others, he treats human beings as a merely physical existence, abstracting the human mind as the subject of 'recognition'. He keeps silent about the human mind when he considers the three subjects — life, life-process, species — which in reality exist as moments of capitalist production. In the abstraction and omission that we find in Hegel's account there are hidden away the capitalist determinations of production, consumption, distribution and exchange.

As we have just seen, the process of capitalist production begins with an exchange between capital and labour-power in order to link the distributed conditions of production which are productively consumed in the production process.

Marx's order of analyșis, 'A. Consumption' to 'B. Distribution' to 'C. Exchange' in the second section of the Introduction to the *Grundrisse*, is in fact the correct analytical order for revealing the capitalist determinations of the four categories which *prima facie* constitute 'production in general'. Exchange, at the end of this progress, is the determination from which capital originates. The essential nature of exchange is shown in the form of circulation, M–C–C′–M′, which signifies an increase in value.

Marx's next task is therefore to inquire just how to demonstrate the genesis of capital, so he considers his method and system or plan. He handles this task in the third section of the Introduction to the *Grundrisse*, but employs a synthetic order — exchange or circulation, then distribution or separation and reconnection, and finally consumption, including industrial and individual — that is contrary to the analytical order in which he considered these categories in the second section.

The method of political economy and 'analytical method, synthetic method, the simple, and classification'

At the beginning of the third section of Marx's Introduction to the *Grundrisse*, 'The method of political economy', we find the following paragraph. It is often cited because in it Marx spoke of ascending and descending methods:

> The economists of the seventeenth century, e.g., always begin with the living whole, with population, nation, state, several states, etc.; but they always conclude by discovering through analysis [*durch Analyse*] a small number of determinant, abstract, general relations such as division of labour, money, value, etc. As soon as these individual moments had been more or less firmly established and abstracted, there began the economic systems, which ascended from the simple [*das Einfache*], such as labour, division of labour, need, exchange-value, to the level of the state, exchange between nations and the world market. The latter is obviously the scientifically [*wissenschaftlich*] correct method (N 100–1, M 36; quotation largely altered).

Here Marx takes William Petty's *Political arithmetick* of 1690 as representative of the economic works of the seventeenth century. Petty compares three superpowers, France, the Netherlands and England. He inquires into the causes of the power of nations and concludes that it lies in the money necessary to employ wage-workers in manufacture. He thus descends from the nation down to money.

For the ascending method Marx turns to Adam Smith's *The wealth of nations* of 1776, in which Smith inquires into the nature and causes of wealth, not merely of Britain, but of all nations, and he demonstrates how the division of labour brings about material abundance even among the middle and lower classes of society. He ascends from the simple category 'division of labour' to exchange, distribution, the accumulation of capital and lastly to the revenue of the state. *The wealth of nations* thus reflects the ascending method.

However, Marx is conscious not only of Petty and Smith, but also of Hegel. This is indicated by Marx's use of Hegel's terminology 'through analysis' and 'the simple' in the quotation above. Moreover when Marx asserts that the systematic method with which we ascend from the abstract or 'the simple' to 'the concrete' or the complex is scientifically correct, he evidently follows Hegel.

Marx's characterisation of the method of the seventeenth-century economists is based on this definition of 'analytical method' by Hegel:

> While finite recognition presupposes *what is distinguished from it* as something already found and confronting it — the various *facts* [*Tatsachen*] of external nature or of consciousness — it has, in the first place, 1. *formal identity* or the *abstraction* of generality [*Allgemeinheit*] for the form of its action. Its activity therefore consists in analysing the given concrete [*das gegebene Konkrete*], isolating its differences, and giving them the form of *abstract generality*. Or it leaves the concrete [*das Konkrete*] as a *ground*, and by setting aside the unessential-looking particulars, brings into relief a concrete general, the *Genus* [*Gattung*] or Force and Law. This is the *analytical method* (sect. 227; quotation largely altered).[6]

According to Marx, the method of the seventeenth-century economists coincides with what Hegel defines as 'analytical method', quoted above. But the method of eighteenth-century economists follows what Hegel calls 'synthetic method', defined as follows:

> The movement of the synthetic method [*synthetische Methode*] is the reverse of the analytical method. The latter starts from the individual [*das Einzelne*], and proceeds to the general [*das Allgemeine*]; in the former the starting-point is given by the

> general (as a *definition*), from which we proceed by particularizing [*Besonderung*] (in *classification*) to the individual (the *theorem*). The synthetic method thus presents itself as the development of the moments of the Notion on the objects (sect. 228, Z; quotation largely altered).[7]

The wealth of nations systematically reflects the synthetic method. It starts from the simplest definition, division of labour or production, and proceeds to exchange, distribution, and reproduction or accumulation of capital. It functions in a spiral because it subsumes definitions which have been posited as presuppositions ('the pre-posited' [*Voraus-Setzung*]). For example, in Book II reproduction develops in the following order: from division of stock or capital (Chapter 1), to division of revenue (Chapter 2), to productive labour (Chapter 3), to profit and interest (Chapter 4), to capital investment (Chapter 5). These themes are considered in a spiral as factors of reproduction.

However, as we can see from the discussion of reproduction in Book II of *The wealth of nations*, Smith does not explicate the determinations of capital, but rather describes them in physical terms as natural or as 'production in general', so he materialises capital-value. Marx criticises 'production in general' as defined in *The wealth of nations* and then redefines it as historically determined. This task also encompasses a critique of Hegel's *Logic*, arguing that both classic authors take capitalist production to be natural. Marx thinks that Smith displays the material aspect of capitalist production, overlooking the formal aspect, whereas Hegel expresses the formal or ideal aspect. He does this in demonstrating the self-creation of the 'idea', which is in fact the value-consciousness characteristic of the bourgeois. In that way the material aspect is subject to the formal. Hegel's *Logic* is the self-creation of the 'idea', but Marx exposes this as capitalist production described from the viewpoint of the capitalist, even though it is described by Hegel as natural.

Marx gives a critical assessment of Hegel's synthetic method:

> The concrete [*das Konkrete*] is concrete because it is the concentration of many determinations, hence unity of the diverse. It appears in the process of thinking [*im Denken*], therefore, as a process of concentration, as a result, not as a point of departure, even though it is the point of departure in reality and hence also the point of departure for intuition [*Anschauung*]

> and conception. Along the first path the full conception was evaporated to yield an abstract determination; along the second, the abstract determinations lead towards a reproduction of the concrete by way of thought. In this way Hegel fell into the illusion of conceiving the real [*das Reale*] as the product of the thought [*Denken*] concentrating itself, probing its own depths, and unfolding itself out of itself, by itself, whereas the method of ascending from the abstract to the concrete is only the way in which thought appropriates the concrete, reproduces it as the spiritually concrete [*als ein geistig Konkretes*]. But this is by no means the process by which the concrete itself comes into being (N 101, M 36; quotation partially altered).

Hegel defines the analytical method as analysing the concrete and finding an abstract general form, while Marx defines 'the first path', i.e. the method of descending from the concrete to the abstract, as the process in which the concrete is dissolved into an abstract determination. What Marx calls 'the first path' is based on Hegel's analytical method.

Hegel says that the synthetic method is 'the development of the moments of the notion', proceeding from the abstract or general and then particularising to the individual instance. Marx calls this 'the method of ascending from the abstract to the concrete'. This order — from the general (*das Allgemeine*) by way of particularising (*Besonderung*) to the individual (*das Einzelne*) instance — represents Hegel's synthetic method. In Marx's work this is reflected in the triadic composition of the 'Chapter on Capital' in the *Grundrisse* as 'I. Generality of Capital', 'II. Particularity of Capital', 'III. Individuality of Capital'.[8]

What Hegel says in 'the development of the moments of the notion' signifies for Marx that reality is mentally reproduced and appropriated as the concrete concept. This is a totality of manifold determinations in the mind, so categories in the Doctrine of Being become presuppositions of the notion of capital, and categories in the Doctrine of Essence develop from generality or the 'notion' itself, towards particularity or judgement, and up to individuality or syllogism. Marx thus turns the two doctrines of the objective logic into objective moments of the mental reproduction of the concrete. This reflects Hegel's triad — generality, particularity, individuality — in the Doctrine of the Notion.

However, Hegel regards the synthetic method as the process in which the real or concrete is posited (*ist gesetzt*), because he thinks that the process of thinking is the same as that of positing something in actuality. He does not distinguish between the two processes. For him, thinking means actualising the real, and therefore the only labour which he recognises is alien, spiritual labour. The *Logic* is the most abstract description of the 'idea', which objectifies itself as the demiurgos of the universe through its spiritual labour.

By contrast Marx insists that the concrete concept, bourgeois society, which he and Hegel take as their object of study, really exists outside the minds of those who think about it. So why has Marx compared his method with Hegel's and in fact praised his synthetic method as scientifically correct? Why, in constructing the 'Chapter on Capital', is Marx applying Hegel's triad of generality, particularity and individuality?

Here Marx intends critically to absorb Hegel's idealism, the idealism through which Hegel unconsciously describes capitalism,[9] in which the ideal subject (value) is dominant. Marx reads the *Logic* as a work in which the ideal subject or 'idea' alienates itself, i.e. posits the concrete or the real, as the social logic of value-consciousness in the person who recognises value in property. The relation of private exchange necessitates a subjective or ideal activity to equate products and to effect their exchange. Because of that, the activity becomes a subject which appears as if it should posit the concrete or the real.

Hegel accepts a reversal of ideas and reality as a natural fact and describes it in the *Logic*. The relations of private property then divide human activity into mental and physical labour, and mental labour rules over physical. Hegel takes alienation in the *Logic* to be natural, because he is ignorant of the fact that alienation is historical *par excellence*. In the *Economic and philosophical manuscripts (1844)* Marx has already detected the perverse character of the *Logic*, writing that Hegel grasps the positive aspect of labour 'within alienation or abstraction'.

Therefore Marx's critique of Hegel's idealism is a critique of pseudo-naturalism and pseudo-historicism. Marx's critical absorption of the *Logic* is one of the important factors in his critique of political economy, and it is to be understood as a reading of the *Logic* as an account of value-consciousness in persons who represent the ideal character of modern private property. Marx's work is supplemented by a critique of the political economy of Smith and Ricardo, who describe material aspects of capitalist production but are indifferent to its ideal aspects, including the drive to self-expansion. This is because these economists unconsciously reify (*versachlichen*) or transubstantiate value-consciousness into material products, and mistake it for what is purely material. In short, Marx reveals the determinations of capital within what the economists treat as a purely material system of production. As Hegel is 'a vulgar idealist', so Smith and Ricardo are 'vulgar materialists' (N 687, M 567; quotation partially altered).

Marx considers where a systematic critique of political economy should start, taking up 'the simplest economic category' (N 101, M 36), i.e. exchange-value, possession (*Besitz*), money, exchange and labour in general, which he derives from Chapter 5 on money of Book I of *The wealth of nations*. He traces them back to their point of departure, inquiring where and how money is generated, and noting that from money comes capital. Accepting Hegel's view that the end of an analysis is the same as the starting point of a synthesis, i.e. 'the simple', Marx confirms this in economic categories. Hegel writes:

> The *general* is in and for itself the first moment of the Notion because it is the *simple* moment, and the particular is only subsequent to it because it is the mediated moment; and conversely the *simple* is the more general, and the concrete, as in itself differentiated and so mediated, is that which already presupposes the transition from a first.[10]

'The general' is simple and abstract enough to develop by mediating particular determinations under itself. 'The concrete' is 'the manifold' or 'the complex' (*das Viel-Fache*), an 'individual' instance, which is composed of particular moments. At first the concrete is abstracted into 'the simple' (*das Ein-Fache*), and then 'the simple' is developed into the 'notion', proceeding from 'the general' by particularisation up to the moments of 'the individual' or 'one determined totality'. Hegel defines 'determinate being' (*Dasein*) or 'what is there' as a reproduction of 'what has already been' (*ge-wesen*) or as the existence of 'essence' (*Wesen*). 'Determinate being' is what has been posited by 'essence'.

Employing this demonstration, Marx argues in economic terms that the product undergoes a transformation into the commodity, the commodity into money, and money into capital. Then capital as subject posits the product, the commodity and money. The first 'determinate beings' (product, commodity and money) are what is posited by the 'essence' (capital). They are forms of existence of capital.

Neither Hegel nor Marx conceives the progress from 'the simple' to 'the complex' in a one-sided way. Rather 'the simple' changes into 'the complex', and then 'the simple' is determined as what 'the complex' has posited. What is at first 'pre-posited' or presupposed (*voraus-gesetzt*) is then posited and reproduced as a result. This forms the circle of 'pre-positing' or presupposition (*Voraus-Setzung*) and 'positing' or 'the posited' (*Setzung*). Therefore once something is 'pre-posited', it is then repeatedly posited as the next 'pre-posited' or presupposition, forming a circulation which looks as if it should exist forever.

The point at which Marx departs from Hegel is his judgement on whether this circulation is merely logical, or whether the first 'pre-positings' or presuppositions were originally manifested in the course of history and then receded as capitalism developed.

Indeed both Hegel and Marx posit 'the general' at the outset, though for each the content is different. Hegel's 'the general' is the 'self-cause' which has no historical origin. It is an eternal subject, whereas Marx's is historical in form, the alienated relation of private exchange. This has become an ideal subject independent of the persons who live within the social relationship of private exchange.

Marx argues that once the logical presupposition is given, it posits the same presupposition as a result, and thus continues to reproduce itself. That is the way an organic system reproduces itself. However, he inquires where the first presuppositions were given, and he finds that they were posited historically. The logical circulation of self-reproduction begins just after the logical presuppositions have been established.

Hegel does not inquire if these logical presuppositions are independent of their historical actuality or not, though he writes a good deal about history, taking the historical subject to be what is natural. His ideal subject or 'idea' is in fact an abstract expression of value. As the demiurgos it posits itself in the *Logic*, it posits nature in the *Philosophy of nature*, and it posits humankind in the *Phenomenology of spirit*.

Marx uses a logico-historical method when he starts to demonstrate that the bourgeois economy is a system which reproduces itself. The first logical presupposition reproduces itself and as a result it generates the next presupposition. Using this demonstration he shows how the first presuppositions were posited in early capitalism: from exchange in the thirteenth century, to manufacture from the sixteenth century onwards, to the industrial revolution from the last half of the eighteenth century, and eventually to the first capitalist crisis in 1825.

'The simple' in Marx's ascending or synthetic method is therefore a presupposition which was posited in history. But at first he takes 'the simple' to be a logical presupposition. It becomes the immanent moment of logical circulation, e.g. the circuit of money-capital and the accumulation of capital in the *Grundrisse*, and on that proof he grounds his account of the historical origin and development of 'the simple' as the primitive community and primitive accumulation. In this demonstration he uses a logico-historical order. Using that methodology he criticises Hegel, who assumes that presupposition and result, or cause and effect, should continue infinitely to form a logical circulation. Hegel does this in his theory of 'positing reflection' and 'causality' in the Doctrine of Essence with respect to the bourgeois economy.

Marx asserts that reproductive circulation was the historical presupposition for the bourgeois economy, and he descends analytically to primitive accumulation. This demonstrates that the value-form generates capital. Capital links the presuppositions or conditions of production, which are separated in primitive accumulation. And it will cease to exist, as Marx argues later, through the annulment of the law of value. This is caused by the development of fixed capital, which leaves disposable time to be enjoyed when human emancipation is achieved.

In short, bourgeois society is not a closed society, but is dependent on the past and open to the future. By contrast Hegel unconsciously describes it in the *Logic* as a closed system which the ideal subject regenerates and reproduces infinitely as its own organism. By reading Hegel's 'idea' as the intersubjective value-consciousness of the bourgeoisie, Marx uncovers the capitalist economy itself in the *Logic*.

Marx reads the *Logic* as the phenomenology or genesis of the value-consciousness described in the 'Chapter on Money' and the 'Chapter on Capital' in the *Grundrisse*. In the 'Chapter on Money' he reveals the way in which this bourgeois consciousness is ideally expressed through the relation of private exchange, which is analogous to Hegel's definition of 'being-for-itself'. This is in fact the relationship of commodity-owners in the market. In the market, value is separated from them through the equation of their commodities, on the presumption that their commodities have equivalent value in the first place. Marx touches on how commodity-exchangers take part in the formation of money without being aware of this equation, and he begins his demonstration of the genesis of money by considering the value-form and the process of exchange. At this point commodity-owners share their value-consciousness intersubjectively in the money in which their consciousness is materialised.

At the beginning of the 'Chapter on Capital' Marx defines capital as the generality which increases value, changing its temporal forms. Through alienated relations, value produces value-consciousness, which mediates capital. Capital-value then posits capitalist consciousness as a capitalist who ideally identifies particular concrete forms of value with an abstract capital-value. The capitalist mediates these concrete forms of value as the incarnation of capital-value in a circular motion.

The capitalist carries on an exchange with the wage-labourer as a private owner with an equal title. However, through this exchange, the capitalist aims at 'form as content', so the form of exchange, which is value, has become its content or purpose. The wage-labourer, who is now subsumed under the process of the production of capital as mere variable capital, must engage in material production, and the wage-labourer is subject to capitalist consciousness, which strives to increase capital-value. As a result, the wage-labourer produces not only surplus-value which belongs to the capitalist, but also a loss of property for wage-labourers themselves. The wage-labourer produces the capital-labour relation, and it becomes evident that capital itself is the accumulation of the surplus labour of wage-labourers. A new consciousness is born as the wage-labourer suspects that capitalist property is against the interests of wage-labourers. In that way commonplace bourgeois consciousness can be broken down and antagonistic consciousness can emerge.

In considering 'disposable time' Marx argues that value-consciousness arises from the exchange-relation of commodities, which is presupposed as the product of 'individual immediate labour'. But in the course of capitalist development, that sort of labour is replaced by 'collective scientific labour'. This arises through technological innovation embodied in machinery or fixed capital. Thus the law of value ceases to operate, because the labour objectified in the product decreases to a minimum. Then capital-value consciousness loses ground and begins to vanish, leaving behind proletarian consciousness. Eventually this develops into a free society.

In that way Marx's phenomenology of spirit is developed in the *Grundrisse*. When he evaluates Hegel's synthetic method as the way to reproduce the real, he does not accept it as a merely formal explanation, but as a real mode of demonstration based on the dramaturgy of the birth and death of value-consciousness. Marx's plan is as follows:

> The classification (*Einteilung*) obviously has to be
> 1. The general, abstract determinations . . .
> 2. The categories which make up the inner structure of bourgeois society and on which the fundamental classes rest. Capital, wage-labour, landed property . . .
> 3. Concentration of bourgeois society in the form of the state . . .
> 4. The international relation of production . . .
> 5. The world market and crisis (N 108, M 43; quotation partially altered).[11]

Marx's discussion of method and 'the simple', followed by his classificatory plan, reflects the order found in Hegel's work in the Doctrine of the Notion: 'The statement of the second moment of the notion, or of the determinateness of the general [*das Allgemeine*] as *particularizing* [*Besonderung*], is *classification* [*Einteilung*] in accordance with some external consideration' (sect. 230; quotation partially altered).[12]

'The simple' at the beginning of systematic explanation is also 'the general' or *differentia specifica*,[13] and it becomes particularised, as is shown in the classification above. After the plan just quoted Marx made other plans in the 'Chapter on Money' (N 227–8, M 151–2) and the 'Chapter on Capital' (N 264, M 187; N 275, M 199). The plans in the 'Chapter on Capital' are clearer. Following Hegel, these plans are composed in the triadic order 'I. Generality of Capital', 'II. Particularity of Capital' and 'III. Individuality of Capital'. This triadic plan is manifested throughout the 'Chapter on Capital' of the *Grundrisse*.

Mode of production and ideology, and 'the absolute idea'

In the fourth and final section of the Introduction to the *Grundrisse*

Marx makes eight notes on the problems he has kept in mind:

1. *War* developed earlier than peace; the way in which certain economic relations such as wage-labour, machinery etc. develop earlier, owing to war and in the armies etc. . . .
2. *Relation of previous ideal historiography to the real. Namely of the so-called histories of culture, which are only histories of religions and states* . . .
3. *Secondary and tertiary* matters; in general, *derivative, inherited*, not original relations of production . . .
4. *Accusations about the materialism of this conception. Relation to naturalistic materialism.*
5. *Dialectic of the concepts productive force (means of production)* and relation of production . . .
6. *The uneven development of material production relative to e.g. artistic development*. In general, the concept of progress not to be conceived in the usual abstractness. Modern art etc. . . . Roman private law . . .
7. *This conception appears as necessary development.* But legitimation of chance. How. (Of freedom also . . .) . . .
8. *The point of departure obviously from the natural characteristic*; . . . (N 109–10, M 43–4; quotation partially altered).

The eight items have already been analysed in detail.[14] For that reason, we mention only their connection with Hegel's *Logic*.

So far in his discussion Marx has reflected Hegel's consideration of individual life, life-process and 'genus' as discussed in 'life' under the 'idea' in the Doctrine of Notion, the last book of the *Logic*. And he has studied method, 'the simple' and classification. After critically reflecting on 'life' and 'recognition' in the first three sections of the Introduction to the *Grundrisse*, Marx takes up the 'absolute idea' in the fourth section.

Following Hegel, who considers such topics as nature and spirit, art and religion, philosophy, 'the beginning', dialectic, system and method in his *Logic*, Marx investigates the bourgeois mode of production in the first three sections of the Introduction to the *Grundrisse*. Then he gropes for his own historical theory of modes of production, applying in the fourth section the summary listed above (first, third and fifth items). The fourth section of the Introduction to the *Grundrisse* evidently fills out Marx's scheme by criticising the 'absolute idea'.

In his Introduction to the *Grundrisse* Marx intends to make use of

Hegel's idealism, which argues the dominance of an ideal subject. This occurs in the Doctrines of Being and of Essence, but as a perverse expression of capitalist production. Marx reveals this logic of modern value-consciousness, and so criticises Hegel's work as ideology.[15]

2
The 'Chapter on Money' and the Doctrine of Being

Product, commodity and money, and 'identity, difference, opposition and contradiction'

As noted in the Preface to the present work, the 'Chapter on Money' in Marx's *Grundrisse* corresponds to the Doctrine of Being in Hegel's *Logic*. However, at the beginning of the 'Chapter on Money' we find the following paragraph, which is written with reference to Hegel's description of 'Identity, Difference, Opposition and Contradiction' at the beginning of the Doctrine of Essence.[1] Marx writes:

> The simple fact that the commodity exists doubly, in one aspect as a specific product whose natural form of determinate being [*natürliche Dasein*] ideally contains (latently contains) its exchange-value (*money*), in which all connection with the natural form of determinate being of the product is stripped away again — this double, *differentiated* existence [*Existenz*] must develop into a *difference* [*Unterschied*], and the difference into *opposition* [*Gegensatz*] and *contradiction* [*Widerspruch*] (N 147, M 81; quotation partially altered).

Why does Marx write in that way? He does so, because he is thinking in the following manner. The identity (*Identität*) of a simple product with itself is differentiated into dual form: 1. the 'natural form of determinate being of the product' (in other words, use-value; in fact Marx refrains from using this term for a reason explained later), and 2. the 'form of exchange-value'. When the product is brought into an exchange-relation it becomes (*werden*) a commodity. When exchange-value, which the commodity-owner pursues, is further realised as money, the immanent difference between use-value and exchange-value becomes an external opposition between commodity and money. As we shall see later, this opposition will develop into a contradiction within money, and from money arises capital. Marx thus links the movement 'from product to commodity to money and on to capital' with the movement 'from identity to difference to opposition and on to contradiction', as Hegel writes in the transition from 'being' to 'essence'.

A commodity cannot simply exist as such, and so money is generated. From money arises capital. In the paragraph cited above, Marx obtains a theoretical perspective on this development. In other words, the product is explicitly defined as a commodity when it is the product of capital, or when capital posits or produces a product. Therefore the commodity is by nature commodity-capital. This means that the product is posited as a commodity through the capital-relation, into which the value-relation has transformed itself. If we inquire why the product exists as such, we must trace it back to capital. 'Positing reflection' (*die setzende Reflexion*) at the beginning of the Doctrine of Essence is the determination which mediates 'being' and 'essence'. 'Determinate being' (*Dasein*) will be revealed as that which 'essence' (*Wesen*) has posited as 'ground' (*Grund*). It is the semblance (*Schein*) of 'essence'.

Using this logic Marx connects the commodity with capital in this way. The commodity as 'determinate being' is in fact the product which capital has posited. Because the product becomes a commodity, the commodity gives rise to money, and money gives rise to capital. But now capital posits the product as a commodity. Therefore the product at the beginning of this analysis is *de facto* that which capital has posited.

For capital, the product as 'the simple' or 'the posited' is a result. The product is thus posited or reproduced at the end in order to become the next presupposition. Marx has obtained this perspective on the circular relationship of presupposition or 'the posited' from Hegel's 'positing reflection'.

Marx grasps the relation between the 'Chapter on Money' and the 'Chapter on Capital' in a similar way. The logical relation between presupposition as 'the simple' or the product, and 'the posited' as 'the complex' or capital, is already established in the Introduction to the *Grundrisse*. This is the logical phase of the logico-historical circulation through which what is historically posited is reproduced as the next presupposition in logic.

Marx uses this methodological perspective in the 'Chapter on Money'. In that work he interprets Hegel's Doctrine of Being as the genesis of the value-consciousness shared amongst the bourgeoisie, in effect a phenomenology of the bourgeois spirit.

The two aspects of the commodity and 'likeness and unlikeness'

At the beginning of the 'Chapter on Money' in the *Grundrisse*, Marx defines the commodity as follows:

> The commodity is neither posited as constantly exchangeable, nor exchangeable with *every other commodity* in its natural properties [*Eigenschaften*]; not in its natural likeness [*Gleichheit*] with itself, but as unlike [*ungleich*] itself, as something unlike [*Ungleiches — sic*] itself, as exchange-value (N 142, M 77; quotation largely altered).

What is 'natural likeness' in the above quotation? Marx uses the word 'natural' as an antonym of 'social'. It means something that is free from social determinations, or free from the commodity–money relation. In other words, historical and social determinations are abstracted from 'natural' ones. Therefore the 'natural likeness' or 'natural properties' of the commodity means use-value or 'the product as such', which people obtain from nature through labour.

So long as the relations of the primitive community persist, human beings as natural force or natural form are directly united with nature itself or natural matter. When members of the community are dissociated into modern individuals, they relate to each other through the exchange of their products. Then the product is no longer a mere natural 'likeness' but becomes a commodity. The product as a commodity is not posited in its natural likeness to itself or as use-value, but as unlike itself or as exchange-value. Its use-value now changes into 'use-value for others', or social use-value.

This two-fold determination of the product as a commodity is based on Hegel's 'pure reflection': 'Likeness [*Gleichheit*] is an Identity only of those things which are *not the same*, not identical with each other; and Unlikeness [*Ungleichheit*] is a *relation* [*Beziehung*] of things that are unlike [*Ungleichen*]' (sect. 118; quotation partially altered).[2]

Both likeness and unlikeness are defined, not in the sense that they are separated and indifferent to each other, but in the sense that they hold each other as their own indispensable element, connected in their own definition. Hegel continues:

> In the case of difference, in short, we like to see identity, and in the case of identity we like to see difference. Within the range of the empirical sciences, however, the one of these two categories is often allowed to put the other out of sight and mind. Thus the scientific problem at one time is to reduce existing differences to identity; on another occasion, with equal one-sidedness, to discover new differences (sect. 118, Z).

Marx does not try to discover a definition of identity without differences, nor one of differences without identity, but one in which both 'likeness' and 'unlikeness' are mutually mediated. He does this in his critique of political economy, one of the typical empirical sciences, by treating it as the self-recognition of bourgeois society. His critique of Hegel also limits the validity of the *Logic* to bourgeois society.

Marx considers in detail how exchange-value is generated and transformed:

> I equate each of the commodities with a third [*ein Drittes*]; i.e. unlike [*ungleich*] themselves. This third, which differs from them both [the two commodities in exchange], exists initially only in the head [of the commodity-owners], as a conception, since it expresses a relation [*ein Verhältnis*]; just as relations in general can only be thought [*gedacht*], when they should be fixed, in distinction from the subjects who relate to each other (N 143, M 77–8; quotation largely altered).

By using Hegel's definition of 'likeness', i.e. the identity of what is not identical, Marx considers commodities on a new level. He calls their 'likeness' exchange-value.

What is exchange-value in reality? Marx thinks that it is the relation of private exchange, which is unconsciously separated from the subjects who form the relation. Exchange-value arises through the action of equating products as commodities. This can occur because of the presumption that an equivalent exchange-value originally exists in each commodity.

The use-value of a commodity for its owner is a non-use-value. Thinking of Adam Smith's explanations of exchange and division of labour in *The wealth of nations*, Marx writes as follows: 'Exchange and division of labour reciprocally condition one another. Since everybody works for himself but his product is nothing [*Nichts*] for him' (N 158, M 91). The commodity-owner brings his product to exchange. Use-value is non-use-value or 'nothing' for the commodity-owner, but it may be a use-value or 'being' for others. Each use-value is different, but in order to be exchanged, each must be equated to another through 'a third'. What is 'the third'? What really exists in the exchange-relation is the use-value of each commodity. Therefore 'the third' can only be another relation through which products with different use-values are linked. This relation exists only in the minds of persons. It is what is thought (*gedacht*).

It is noteworthy that the relation of 'the third' comes to exist only when persons, who relate to each other, keep it in mind. However, they do not notice this mental action. Though they form the relation of commodity-exchangers, they presume that exchange-value exists originally in a commodity, without an awareness that exchange-value derives from an unconscious reflection of the real exchange-relation between their products. Exchange-value is a relation which is abstracted unawares from exchange and transformed into an immanent factor of the commodity itself. In that way the real exchange-relation is alienated as exchange-value from the exchangers and is materialised in the commodity.

In writing the sentences quoted above, Marx is surely remembering the following passage from Hegel:

> Difference is 1. *immediate* difference, i.e. *diversity* [*Verschiedenheit*]. In diversity each of the different things *is by itself* what it is, and is indifferent to its relation to any other. This relation is therefore external to it. Because of the indifference of the diverse things to the difference between them, the difference falls outside them into a third [*ein Drittes*], *something comparable* [*Vergleichendes*] (sect. 117; quotation largely altered).[3]

Hegel does not explain 'the third' any further, but Marx assumes that it is the value-consciousness of commodity-owners, which they unconsciously project on to their products and take to be an original feature of the commodity itself.

The commodity-owner and 'ideality of being-for-itself'

In bourgeois society a person must engage in a metabolism with nature through the commodity–money relation. The private nature of this process requires a person to perform this practice by identifying products with 'the third', exchange-value. This is because the private exchange of products, which are different in use-value from each other, is realised through an equation. In that equation the exchange-relation is separated as exchange-value from the persons who form the relationship. This equation is a determination (*Bestimmung*) of the commodity-owner whose 'final cause' is speculation in terms of value, a form of alienated thinking and behaviour.

'Being-for-itself' (*Fürsichsein*) in Hegel's *Logic* is concerned with just this matter. 'Determinate being' (*Dasein*) becomes 'being-for-itself' (*Fürsichsein*) when it is defined as 'something' (*Etwas*) in relation to another 'determinate being', 'another something' (*anderes Etwas*). It is 'being-for-itself' or 'something' that relates to 'another something' and determines itself in relation to it. Hegel writes:

> In Being-for-itself enters the determination of *ideality* [*Idealität*]. *Determinate being* has *reality* [*Realität*] in the first instance when it is apprehended only in its being or affirmation (sect. 91); and thus even finiteness in the first instance is in the determination of reality (sect. 95; quotation largely altered).[4]

Hegel derives 'being-for-itself' from the relation between 'something' and 'another something'. 'Being-for-itself' is the relation that is ideal *par excellence*, i.e. 'being-for-itself' is ideality which mediates the reality of 'determinate being' or 'something'.

However, Hegel neither inquires into what actually causes the relation between 'something' and 'another something', nor asks why the reality of 'being-for-itself' cannot subsist as such and must descend into ideality. By contrast Marx investigates the cause, because the ideality in question is the specific characteristic of modern private property.

What Hegel calls 'reality' are the natural attributes and identity of a product when it is observed from the standpoint of political economy. It is 'value in use', in Smith's terminology, material wealth obtained through the metabolic process with nature by 'toil and trouble'. The product cannot continue to exist as mere use-value when it is brought into the relation of private exchange.

What Hegel calls 'ideality' is the abstraction which exchangers keep in mind in equating their products. They form an exchange-relation and abstract the real 'unlikeness' of their products into an ideal 'likeness', in short, exchange-value.

Marx thus interprets the reality of 'determinate being' and the ideality of 'being-for-itself' as use-value and exchange-value respectively. A product has those two factors because the process of metabolism between human beings and nature is carried on through a separation and reintegration in the course of private exchange.

Marx also criticises Hegel directly:

> This symbol [money], this material sign of exchange-value, is a product of exchange itself, and not the execution of an idea conceived *a priori* (N 144, M 79).
>
> These *objective* dependency relations [*diese sachlichen Abhängigkeitsverhältnisse*] also appear, in opposition to those of *personal* dependence . . . in such a way that individuals are now ruled by *abstractions* [*Abstraktionen*], whereas earlier they depended on one another. The abstraction, or idea [*Idee*], however, is nothing more than the theoretical expression of those material relations which are their master [*Herr*]. Relations can be expressed, of course, only in ideas . . . (N 164, M 96).[5]

Marx reinterprets Hegel's 'idea'. He sees it as an abstraction which private persons unconsciously but inevitably generate as an equalising factor when they relate to each other in an exchange of products or in 'objective dependency'. He thinks that the subject in bourgeois society is in fact not the 'idea', but the commodity-relation or form of the commodity. Hegel's 'idea' is an abstract expression of this relation.

For Marx the 'propensity to exchange', which Adam Smith emphasised in human nature, has become an axiom for the bourgeoisie. They live within the commodity-relation or 'commercial society'. Exchange-value is what they express ideally in the commodity-relation, their 'final cause'. The productive ability which is bestowed on human beings in history is alienated in practice and then defined so as to express exchange-value, an ideality. Hegel mistakes this ideality for the 'idea', the demiurgos of the universe.

The bourgeoisie are conscious of exchange-value in the form of prices, so their consciousness is determined as value-consciousness. But at this level they presume that exchange-value as infinity (*Unendlichkeit*) is immanent within the product as finiteness (*Endlichkeit*). Marx's work relates to this comment by Hegel: 'The truth of the finite is rather its *ideality*' (sect. 95).

The product (finiteness) is determined so that it is equated (like, *gleich*) through an ideal 'third' with its reality as a use-value (unlikeness, *Ungleichheit*). In the sentence above Hegel asserts that the product becomes a commodity in private exchange. The commodity is then determined not only as use-value (finiteness or reality), but as exchange-value (infinity or ideality). Unawares he describes a situation in which people must express their private interests in a specific way. He presumes the situation to be natural, although in fact it is historically established.

Marx sees the two aspects of the commodity — use-value and exchange-value — in Hegel's definitions of 'reality of determinate being' and 'ideality of being-for-itself'. He criticises the pseudo-naturalism expressed in Hegel's Doctrine of Being, and he argues that this pseudo-naturalism is shared by the political economists. He does not criticise Hegel's idealism transcendentally, but sees within it an ideal expression of private, alienated activity, the social form of private production.

Money-subject and 'substance as subject'

In the 'Chapter on Money' in the *Grundrisse* Marx finds the genesis of money in a circulation of commodities and money. He attempts to do this by appealing to a contradiction within money itself, though, as we will see later, he touches on the value-form and the process of circulation.

Marx focuses on two aspects of the commodity, 'natural likeness' and 'exchange-value'. However, as noted above, some readers of the 'Chapter on Money' are embarrassed by the fact that he refrains from using the popular term 'use-value', even though he often uses the opposite term 'exchange-value'. No doubt he was well acquainted with the term 'use-value'. Nevertheless he uses other terms instead, e.g. 'natural properties' (*die natürliche Eigenschaften*), 'natural existence' (*die natürliche Existenz*), 'natural determinate being' (*das natürliche Dasein*) etc. (N 141, M 76).

What is Marx's intention in adopting this terminology? He evidently aims to consider the genesis of money using terms found in the works of Aristotle, one of the first thinkers to examine money. At the beginning of the theoretical sections of the 'Chapter on Money' in the *Grundrisse* (N 140, M 75), he puts the 'individual' thing (*Individuum*)[6] (N 235, M 158) or '*a tangible thing*' (*ein handgreifliches Ding*) (N 263, M 187) on the agenda as 'the product'. He calls it 'substance' in the sense of 'primary substance' (*prōtē ousia*) mentioned by Aristotle. Aristotle distinguishes the primary from the secondary substance (*deuterai ousiai*):

> It follows, then, that substance has two senses, a. the ultimate substratum, which is no longer predicated of anything else, and b. that which is a 'this' and separable [*chōriston*] — and of this nature is the shape [*morphē*] or form [*eidos*] of each thing.[7]

Marx considers exchange-value with reference to Aristotle's secondary substance. The commodity thus consists of the primary or natural substance and the secondary substance, exchange-value. The commodity is the concrete instantiation (*synolon*) of the two substances. As mentioned above, the secondary substance is 'separable' (*chōriston, abrennbar*),[8] (*abgetrennt*).[9] Aristotle does not stipulate whether the separable substance or form (*eidos*) is natural or social. Marx comprehends it as social *par excellence*. In actuality it is the relation of exchange separated as exchange-value from persons who relate to each other in a specific way. It is materialised in a product, which thus becomes a commodity. Exchange-value is also separable from the primary substance or matter of the commodity. Marx writes:

> Besides its existence in the commodity, exchange-value gained a proper existence in money, was separated [*getrennt*] from its [natural] substance exactly because the natural determinateness of this substance contradicted its general determination as exchange-value (N 150–1, M 84; quotation largely altered).

What is termed 'its [exchange-value's] substance' in the quotation above is the 'natural substance' in which exchange-value exists. It is in fact use-value. Use-values are 'the material bearers [*Träger*] of . . . exchange-value'.[10] Use-value should not be mistaken for 'abstract human labour', the *social* substance of value.

In the 'Chapter on Capital' we find a similar usage of the term substance: 'the substance in which it [capital] exists'. Here substance refers to particular forms of some natural substance, e.g. the substance of money, commodities, and conditions of production through which capital-value is mediated. Marx uses the word substance, instead of use-value, because he intends to grasp the commodity as a contradiction between primary substance and exchange-value.

Marx states that the two determinations of the commodity contradict each other. 'Contra-diction' means that the commodity contains two contrary aspects. The commodity as a whole is determined as a natural substance, and at the same time as exchange-value. Both aspects are true of it, but mutually exclusive. They then form a contradiction. How is the contradiction resolved or 'dissolved'? Marx answers:

> This contradiction can be dissolved only by objectifying it: i.e. by positing the commodity in a double form, first in its natural, immediate form, then in its mediated form, as money. The latter is possible only because a particular commodity becomes, as it were, the general substance of exchange-values [*die allgemeine Substanz der Tauschwerte*], or because the exchange-values of commodities become identified with a particular commodity different from all others (N 168, M 100; quotation partially altered).

Here in the *Grundrisse* Marx makes a distinction between contradictions that can be transcended and those that are merely represented in another form (N 123, M 58).[11] The contradiction mentioned above belongs to the latter category, because it generates a form in which it is represented. The exchange-value of all commodities becomes separated and independent from the original natural substances in which it has existed, and exchange-value is eventually expressed in the particular natural substance of one money-commodity. Exchange-values are founded on their own particular substances, but in the money-commodity they are represented within one specific substance which possesses natural attributes adequate for fulfilling certain needs. These attributes include unchangeability (inoxidizability) (N 166, M 98), separability, recompoundability and transportability.[12]

This representation is realised through the practice of commodity-owners. They equate the exchange-values of their commodities with a particular natural substance in one commodity such as gold or silver. This common action makes the commodity 'the general substance' in which the exchange-values of all commodities are expressed, to which they are transferred, and in which they exist. One commodity thus becomes money. The theoretical contradiction in the commodity between its two aspects is resolved through the unconscious practice of commodity-owners in generating a form — money — through which the contradiction is represented.

Marx analyses the situation in which the exchange-values of commodities become separated and are expressed in the particular natural substance of one commodity — money. He uses two categories — alienation (*Entfremdung*) and reification (*Versachlichung*):

> — it is clear to the economists that the existence of money presupposes the reification [*Versachlichung*] of the social connection . . . But why do they [people] have faith in the thing [*Sache*]? Indeed obviously [they have faith in the thing] only as a *reified relation* between persons [*als versachlichtem Verhältniss der Personen unter einander*] . . . and it [money] can have a social attribute [*Eigenschaft*], only because the individuals have alienated [*haben entfremdet*] their own social relation as an object from themselves (N 160, M 93; quotation largely altered).

Although in the citation above, the two categories — reification and alienation — suggest a progression from reification to alienation, the order in which the two phenomena occur in reality is the opposite — alienation to reification. '. . . a mutual relation between people's productive activities' (N 160, M 93) appears separated and independent from the human subjects in the exchange-relation, because their practice mutually equates their products as equivalents. The exchangers can equate them in this way because there is a presupposition that their general or abstract labour is objectified in them as the substance of value. Through this practice the exchange-relation between 'private' individuals is separated and becomes independent as exchange-value. Marx calls this separation the alienation (*Entfremdung*) through which the exchange-relation is abstracted from the human subjects who form it.

The sense of the word alienation is the same as in the *Economic and philosophical manuscripts (1844)*. In those manuscripts Marx criticises Hegel, remarking that he grasps human labour 'within alienation' or 'within abstraction' in a way similar to the political economists. Marx's early critique refers to a situation in which money is generated through the unconscious and pervasive practice undertaken by commodity-owners in alienating or abstracting their own relationship as exchange-value. These exchangers bring their products into exchange as commodities, because they consciously believe that they have exchange-value. Thus their unconscious practice in alienating their own relation as exchange-value appears in reverse in their consciousness. In that way their commodities seem to have exchange-value themselves, because the exchangers are confident that their products are the phenomenal form of value itself. Marx is perhaps recalling a similar analysis in Hegel's *Phenomenology of spirit*:

> The *cultivated* [*gebildete*] self-consciousness which traversed the world of the self-alienated Spirit has, through its exteriorization [*Entäusserung*], produced the Thing [*das Ding*] as its own self; therefore, it still retains its own self in it and knows that the Thing lacks self-subsistence, that it is *essentially* only a *being-for-an-other*; or, to give complete expression to the *relation* [*Verhältnis*], i.e., to what alone constitutes the nature of the object here, the Thing counts for it as something that *exists on its own account*; it declares sense-certainty to be absolute truth, but this *being-for-itself* is itself declared to be a moment that merely vanishes and passes over into its opposite, into a being that is at the disposal of an 'other'.[13]

The parenthesis 'money' (*Geld*), inserted by Marx in his excerpts from the *Phenomenology*, is evidence that he understands that Hegel's 'the thing' (*das Ding*), to which self-consciousness relates, is not a mere thing but a commodity: 'When it [the spirit] declares that what it does, it does out of a conviction of duty, this utterance is the *validating* (money) [*das Gelten* (*Geld*)] of its *action*.'[14]

Marx reads the utterance (*Spruch*) of the 'spirit' as economic action, and the validating of its action (*das Gelten seines Handeln*) as money. In fact its utterance is an expression of economic value,[15] because the 'spirit' is that of commodity-owners who unconsciously alienate their own relation from themselves as exchange-value, and then become its mediators. They bear value-consciousness, though they do not recognise how it is formed. In that way Marx analyses the pervasive value-consciousness of commodity-owners by using Hegel's concept 'self-consciousness' from the *Phenomenology*.

Marx brings reification (*Versachlichung*) into focus by moving from alienation to exchange-value. Exchange-value is itself invisible and intangible, so therefore: 'As a general object, it can exist only symbolically . . .' (N 168, M 99). Exchange-value must then be represented in 'the thing' (*Sache*) or 'body' (*Körper*) of a particular commodity, which is the most adequate way for it to be expressed. Marx describes the materialisation of alienated (*entfremdet*) value in 'the thing' or 'body', its 'reification' (*Veraschlichung*) or 'embodiment' (*Verkörperung*) (N 142, M 77). This process, in which the human subjects in a relation of commodity-exchange posit value 'through abstraction' (N 142, M 77)[16] or through alienation, proceeds simultaneously with the process in which they lose their subjectivity. They are unconsciously engaged in the abstraction of value and in the identification of it with 'the thing' (*Sache*) or 'body' (*Körper*). Unawares they generate money through their common action, and they become subject to it. Money is their alienated intersubjectivity reified in a particular natural substance as gold or silver, which is now 'the general substance' of exchange-value. Later in *Capital* Marx defines money, generated in this way, as a 'materialisation' (*Materiatur*)[17] in which value, i.e. a social form, is expressed in a specific natural substance or matter. In Aristotle's terms the secondary substance (*eidos*, form) becomes separated (*chōriston*) from the primary or original substance, and is incarnated in another primary substance. Marx writes: 'Money is the objective medium [*das sachliche Medium*] into which exchange-values are dipped, and in which they obtain the shape [*Gestalt*] corresponding to their general determination' (N 167, M 99; quotation partially altered).

Money as an objective medium or 'objective expression' (*der sachliche Ausdruck*) (N 169, M 100) is 'the money-subject' (*das Geldsubjekt*) (N 167, M 99, etc.) or 'the subject of money' (*das Subjekt des Geldes*) (N 173, M 104). The relation of commodity-exchange is alienated as value from the human subjects who form the relation, and value is materialised in a particular natural substance such as gold or silver. A specific commodity thus becomes 'the money-subject': 'It arises from the essence of exchange-value itself that one particular commodity appears as the money-subject to the money-attribute [*die Geldeigenschaft*] of all commodities' (N 167, M 98–9; quotation largely altered).

> This much arises from what has been developed so far: A particular product (*commodity*) (material) must become the subject of money, which exists as the attribute of every exchange-value. The subject in which this symbol is represented is not a matter of indifference, since the claims to the representing subject are contained in the conditions — conceptual determinations, determinate relations — of what is to be represented (N 173–4, M 104; quotation partially altered).

Within the relation of commodity-exchange people unconsciously lose their subjectivity and become subordinate to money as a subject. The exchange-relation is separated as value, because they abstract it unawares. This abstraction is objectified and identified with a particular substance, so it appears as the money-subject. By tracing the genesis of money as a subject, Marx has clarified why a specific substance, such as gold or silver, becomes the money-subject, and why there exists the fetishism that gold is money by nature. Using this critique, he reveals the real ground of Hegel's thesis that 'substance' is 'subject'. Hegel writes:

> It is out of this judgement [*Ur-Teil* = original division] that the Idea is *in the first place* only the one general *substance* [*Substanz*]; but its developed and true actuality is to be as *subject* [*Subjekt*] and thus as spirit [*Geist*] (sect. 213; quotation largely altered).

In the *Economic and philosophical manuscripts (1844)* Marx argues that Hegel's 'substance' is 'the alienation' (logically: from the infinite, the abstractly general) or 'the absolute and fixed abstraction'.[18] The most crucial category in Hegel's thesis is 'the *spiritual* relationship' (*das geistige Verhalten*)[19] or 'the abstractly spiritual (labour)' (*die abstrakt geistige* [*Arbeit*]),[20] through which 'substance' as 'knowing' (*Wissen*) becomes 'subject'. The labour which Hegel recognises is merely 'to know' (*wissen*). In the *Economic and philosophical manuscripts (1844)* Marx writes that for Hegel, 'Knowing is its [consciousness's] only objective relationship [*Verhalten*].'[21] For Hegel 'knowing' knows itself, and consciousness is therefore self-consciousness. Self-consciousness confirms that everything exists in 'knowing' by objectifying itself as a subject. What appears as an object to self-consciousness (phenomenological knowledge) is nothing but self-consciousness in the form of its own object-consciousness.

In the *Economic and philosophical manuscripts (1844)* Marx reveals that Hegel's 'substance' in the *Phenomenology* is in fact the alienated relation of commodity-ownership as 'value in potentiality' (*an sich*). In other words Hegel has read into 'substance' a specific economic situation in which the commodity-owner reifies value-consciousness in the product. Marx grasps that Hegel's 'self-consciousness' is 'only abstractly conceived man, man produced by abstraction'. 'Man *is* selfish', or an '*abstract egoist*'.[22] 'Man' is the commodity-owner.

For Marx, Hegel's 'object-consciousness' or 'thingness' (*Dingheit*) is reified egoism or value-consciousness. According to Hegel, 'object-consciousness' is '*exteriorized self-consciousness*'[23] or 'an abstract thing, a thing of abstraction'.[24] The abstract thing which the commodity-owner reifies is expressed by Marx in the *Economic and philosophical manuscripts (1844)* as 'money, as the existing and active notion of value',[25] or 'the *money* of Spirit' (*das Geld des Geistes*). Marx calls the reification of value by commodity-owners in their consciousness 'thingness' (*Dingheit*), using one of Hegel's terms. This 'reification' (*Versachlichung*) is value which appears in a thing, and is value-consciousness reflecting on the product, its property.

In Hegel's view 'substance', which becomes 'subject' through self-objectification or self-knowing, is ideal and abstract, whereas Marx mentions only the concrete natural substance. Aware of this limitation, he introduces another category — labour-time:

> Money is labour-time as general object, or the reification of general labour-time, labour-time as *general commodity*. It therefore looks very simple that, while labour-time regulates exchange-values, it is indeed not only the inherent measure of exchange-values, but also their substance itself [*ihre Substanz selbst*] (for, as exchange-values, commodities have no other substance, no natural attribute) . . . (N 168–9, M 100; quotation largely altered).

Marx defines labour-time as the substance of exchange-value. A little later he calls the new category a 'social substance' (*die gesellschaftliche Substanz*) (N 207, M 135), distinguished from 'natural substance' (*die natürliche Substanz*) (N 206, M 134). Using these basic terms, he is able to demonstrate that social substance as 'general labour' (*die allgemeine Arbeit*) (N 205, M 134) is reified in the products of concrete labour through the separation of the exchange-relation as value. This happens through the unconscious actions of commodity-owners. Through this common practice the values of commodities are embodied and reified in a particular natural substance such as gold or silver, which thus appears as the money-subject. Hegel's argument that 'substance' becomes 'subject' is understood by Marx in economic terms as the reification of an alienated relationship. This reification is value embodied in a particular natural substance. That substance, the materialisation of value-consciousness, appears as the money-subject.

Price and 'quantum'

After using Hegel's work in describing the transformation of products into commodities and the transformation of commodities into money, Marx defines 'price' as follows:

> *Exchange-value*, *posited in the determinateness* [*Bestimmtheit*] *of money*, is *price*. Exchange-value is expressed in price as a certain quantum [*Quantum*] of money. Money as price appears first of all as the *unity* [*Einheit*] of all the exchange-values; secondly, it appears as the unit [*Einheit*] of which they all contain a given amount [*Anzahl*], so that the equation with money expresses the quantitative determinateness of exchange-values, their quantitative relation to one another (N 189, M 120; quotation partially altered).[26]

In writing the above passage Marx is evidently recalling the following sentences in Hegel's work on 'quantum' under 'quantity' in his Doctrine of Being:

> In *number* [*Zahl*] the quantum [*Quantum*] reaches its development and perfect determinateness. Number has the one as its element, and contains in itself *amount* [*Anzahl*] according to the moments of discretion, and *unit* [*Einheit*] according to the

moments of continuity, as its qualitative moments (sect. 102).[27]

Both paragraphs cited above share certain terms such as 'quantum', 'unity' and 'amount'. And there is another common characteristic: 'quantum' is put on the same logical level as 'unity' and 'amount'. At the end of his discussion of 'quality', Hegel explains that 'being-for-itself', or 'determinate being', which determines itself in relation to others, tends to express itself as one (*Eins*) through others, 'the many' (*viele Eins*), as much as possible. At an extreme, each 'one', which has taken on the role of the objective material in which the subjective expresses itself, wants to express itself with the 'many' others as an equal subject. Then the 'many' repulse the 'one'. No 'one' can find any difference between itself and the 'many', because they are the same as the 'one'. Therefore they are a reflection of the 'one' itself. The relation of 'one' to 'many' is but a relation of 'one' to itself. Each 'one' of 'many' mutually attracts the others, so 'quality' abstracts itself into 'quantity' — the transition from quality to quantity.

Using the logical relations between 'one and many' and 'repulsion and attraction', Marx demonstrates that money is generated from the commodity-relation. Then using 'quantum' from the conception of 'quantity' in the *Logic*, he defines price, assuming that money is already given as a presupposition.

Hegel writes: '*Quantum*; limited quantity' (sect. 101). Marx notes that the commodity has value in a limited quantity or quantum. It is expressed using money in a certain amount, and thus expresss a price. Every value is expressed only with money, so in that sense money is unity. Money has both a particular quality and a fixed quantity, i.e. a unit, and it is thus composed of a certain amount. Money's first function is to measure the value of the commodity.

Value-form and the process of exchange, and 'one and many'

Marx progresses from the first determination of money as measure of value to its second determination as means of circulation and realiser of prices. Those two determinations of money are both based on the first type of circulation: Commodity — Money — Money — Commodity (C–M–M–C). He writes:

> At first sight, circulation appears as a *badly infinite process* [*ein schlecht unendlicher Process*]. The commodity is exchanged for money, money is exchanged for the commodity, and this is repeated endlessly. This constant renewal of the same process indeed forms an essential [*wesentlich*] moment of circulation. But, viewed more precisely, it reveals other phenomena as well; the phenomena of completion, or, the return of the point of departure into self. The commodity is exchanged for money; money is exchanged for the commodity (N 197, M 126–7; quotation partially altered).

The passage cited above is based on the definition of 'becoming' (*Werden*) and the 'bad infinity' in Hegel's *Logic*:[28] 'Something becomes an other; but the other is itself a something; therefore it likewise becomes an other, and so on *ad infinitum*' (sect. 93; quotation partially altered).

> This *infinity* is the *bad* or *negative* infinity: it is only a negation of a finite: but the finite arises again the same as ever, and is never transcended. In other words, this infinite only expresses the *ought* [*Sollen*] of transcendence of the finite (sect. 94; quotation partially altered).

Marx sees the 'bad infinity' in the formal process C – M – M – C. As long as it appears as an endless, purposeless process, the first commodity is *prima facie* the same as the last. However, if we connect selling (C – M) with purchasing (M – C), it becomes apparent that the hidden purpose of the process consists in the consumption of the use-value of the second commodity outside the process of circulation itself. The process is merely a means. Within this process of circulation, money is determined firstly as a measure of the value of a commodity and secondly as a means of circulation.

Hegel defines the 'bad infinity' as an endless process of renewal between one finiteness and another, or between 'something' and 'another something', forming a contradiction between finitudes to be superseded up to infinity. In what Hegel calls the 'bad infinity' Marx traces the actions of obtaining use-value in the process of circulation and consuming it outside the economic process.

With reference to Hegel, Marx then defines circulation as a continuous movement which has its own purpose:[29] 'It is in the nature of circulation [*Kreislauf*] that every point appears simultaneously as a starting-point and as an ending-point' (N 203, M 132; quotation partially altered). Hegel calls this circulation 'the veritable infinite', which forms a circulation. Its ending-point is connected with the next starting-point. He defines 'the veritable infinite' as follows: '. . . the veritable [*wahrhaft*] infinite, which rather consists in being with itself in its other, or, if enunciated as a process, in coming to itself in its other' (sect. 94, Z; quotation partially altered).[30]

Does the form of circulation $C_1-M-M-C_2$ correspond to the veritable infinite? This form helps to obtain use-value for individual consumption which is realised outside the economic process. Therefore it is defined neither as 'being with itself in its other', nor 'as process . . . coming to itself in its other'.

What is the economic form which matches the true infinite? It is the opposite type of circulation $M_1-C-C-M_2$. What is the purpose of the second type of circulation? Circulation begins with money (M_1) and ends in money, the same thing (M_2). There is no qualitative difference between the beginning and the end, but a quantitative distinction, i.e. $M_2-M_1=\Delta M$, which Marx later calls 'surplus-value' (*Mehrwert*) (N 315, M 233). M_2 is taken to be more than M_1, and M_2 will then immediately return as the next M_1. If $M_2<M_1$, then money vanishes, and the second form of circulation cannot subsist. Money increases endlessly, bringing surplus-value as a result. The purpose of this process is 'form as content', i.e. a content into which the type of circulation — the circulation of value — has changed. Money in the second type of circulation has that special purpose.

However, money is nothing but a particular form (as is the commodity) of increasing value. The general subject here is a process of increasing value, so it is abstract. Commodity and money are particular concrete forms within which the abstract subject maintains itself, metamorphosing from one form to another. Not only the commodity but even money descends to 'finiteness', subject to the 'true infinity' or increasing value. In that way Marx grounds Hegel's abstract definition of the 'true infinity' on economic actuality.

Marx then touches on the third determination of money as 'hoard' or 'treasure' (*Schatz*). This is analysed in detail in the next section of the present work. Here Marx inquires how money generates and tries to solve the problem of the value-form in conjunction with the process of exchange. He does this with reference to the 'true infinity' or endless circulation.

Marx analyses an equivalent relation between simple commodities that lies beneath the definition of money as measure of value:

> If I say a pound of cotton is worth 8d., then I am saying that 1 pound of cotton = 1/116 oz. of gold (the ounce at £3.17s.7d.) (913d.) . . . This original relation of the pound of cotton with gold, by means of which the quantity of gold contained in an ounce of cotton is determined, is fixed by the quantity of labour-time realized in one and the other, the real common substance of exchange-values [*die wirkliche Gemeinsame (sic) Substanz der Tauschwerte*] (N 203–4, M 132).

Where in actual fact are the commodity and money (which Marx takes ultimately to be gold) reduced to labour-time as 'the real common substance of exchange-values' or 'social substance' (N 207, M 135)? Marx presumes that the reduction is realised in the bourgeois economy itself.

> Competition equates the other working days with that one [a definite amount of gold — HU], *modificandis modificatis*. Directly or indirectly. In a word, in the direct production of gold, a definite quantity of gold directly appears as product and hence as the value, the equivalent, of a definite amount of labour-time (N 204, M 132).

Competition abstracts from the natural attributes of commodities and money (gold) in order to equate them with the labour-time necessary to produce them. This is abstraction *in actu*. The market where the abstraction is actualised has been formed in practice:

> The form of barter in which the overflow [*Überfluss*][31] of one's own production is exchanged by chance for that of others is only the *first occurrence* of the product as exchange-value in general, and is determined by accidental needs, whims, etc. But if it should happen to continue, to become a continuing act which contains within itself the means of its renewal, then little by little, from the outside and likewise by chance, regulation of reciprocal exchange arises by means of regulation of reciprocal production, and the costs of production, which ultimately resolve into labour-time, would thus become the measure of exchange. This shows how exchange comes about, and the exchange-value of the commodity (N 204–5, M 133).

Competitive relationships in bourgeois society are traced back to an original, accidental relation in the exchange of surplus products between communities. If this accidental relation stimulates a division of labour within communities, their surplus product turns into the means of their own reproduction, and they thus prodùce more surplus product in terms of use-value, even exchanging part of the product of necessary labour. The reciprocal production and exchange of surplus products between communities is gradually repeated in frequency and regularity. The exchange-relation then penetrates communities and changes them into commodity-producing societies.

Marx has defined the process of exchange in logic and history. His next task is to clarify the logical rule which the owner of a commodity unconsciously follows in the practical process of exchange. What is it? What is it grounded on? Marx now demonstrates the value-form or the genesis of money. Here in the *Grundrisse* he is able to undertake a basic analysis of the value-form, making critical use of Hegel's logic of 'one and many'. At the end of Hegel's discussion of 'determinate being' in the *Logic*, 'being' is defined as what has become independent or 'something' (*Etwas*), and it is distinguished from an independent 'other' (*ein Anderes*). The 'other' is 'an other something' and is but 'something' itself, to which it relates negatively. Therefore the relation of 'something' to 'other' is a relation of self-reflection. 'Being' is thus defined as 'being-for-itself' (*Fürsichsein*). 'Something' is then defined as 'one' and 'an other', i.e. 'something' has become two, two then four. Thus 'one' becomes 'many'. Each of the 'many' is also 'one', the 'many' are many 'ones'. Hegel writes:

> The One . . . just excludes itself and posits itself as the Many. Each of the Many is, however, itself one One. As it behaves as such, so herewith this all-round repulsion converts into its opposition, *attraction* (sect. 97, Z; quotation largely altered).[32]

What sort of image does Hegel have in mind in 'being-for-itself' when it repulses and attracts itself? In fact the real image is as follows:

> We have the readiest instance of Being-for-itself in the *I* [*Ich*]. We know ourselves as existents [*daseiend*], first of all, distinguished from other existents and related thereto. But we also come to know that this width [*Breite*] of determinate being

> [*Dasein*] is sharpened, as it were, to the simple form [*einfache Form*] of Being-for-itself. When we say *I*, it is the expression of infinity and, at the same time, negative self-relation (sect. 96, Z; quotation largely altered).[33]

Here we have the modern individual. Hegel imagines modern persons, who mutually repulse and attract, as dependent on their social relations, though they think they are independent. They cannot live without social intercourse. Through competition and dependency they transcend their exclusive 'finite I' for the 'infinite we'. Hegel thinks that their intersubjectivity is expressed in a simple form, but does not explain it further in the *Logic*.

However in his early note, *First philosophy of spirit* (1803–4), not known to Marx, Hegel considers the actual situation of 'one and many' in the economic relations which inevitably generate money as a simple form:

> *This manifold* labouring at needs as things must likewise realize their concept, their abstraction; their general concept must become a thing like them, but one which, qua universal, represents all needs; *money* is this materially existing concept, the form of unity, or of the possibility of all things needed.[34]

Therefore it is possible to say that when Hegel writes 'a simple form' in the *Logic*, he holds the more concrete image of money as 'the form of unity'. This image derives from his critical reading of Adam Smith's *The wealth of nations*, where Smith explains that the real measure of exchange is labour, 'an abstract notion'. Subsequently Smith writes of it as 'a plain and palpable object', i.e. money was introduced by 'persons of prudence'. Hegel finds a crucial gap between labour as a real measure and money as a convenience, and tries to fill the gap with a view or recognition of money as 'the form of unity' which exists as 'the general' in a material thing and represents all needs. However, Hegel is not successful in demonstrating why and how labour is abstracted, and how abstract labour develops into money, though he writes that 'this manifold labouring at needs [division of labour]' must realise the general concept in a material thing.

Although writing in ignorance of Hegel's critique of Smith's theory of money in the *First philosophy of spirit*, Marx finds social reality in Hegel's 'simple form' and reveals that 'being-for-itself' is not a natural phenomenon but relates to historically-determined persons in specific social relationships.

Marx sees natural substance or use-value in Hegel's definition of 'reality of determinate being', and he sees exchange-value in Hegel's 'ideality of being-for-itself'. Independent persons (*daseiend*) in bourgeois society exist as commodity-owners who use these determinations. A commodity-owner exists 'in himself' (*an sich*) as a 'finite I', which corresponds to the immediate existence of the commodity as a product or natural substance. However, the commodity-owner must form the relation of commodity-exchange with other persons, through and in which 'he' supersedes 'finitude as I' for 'infinity as we'. The individual commodity-owner now shares this intersubjectivity with others in commodity-relations.

Marx associates Smith's image of the person as an economic subject with Hegel's definitions of 'determinate being' and 'being-for-itself'. Smith thinks that 'man' is born with the propensity to exchange given by nature which fixes a certain division of labour.[35] Smith insists that this inevitably results in civilised society or commercial society, which is in fact capitalism.

This naturalistic image of capitalism is also found in Hegel. He has the same kind of image, confusing what is specific to capitalism with what is common to all forms of society. In the 'Minor Logic' he writes as follows:

> The distinction between Nature and Spirit [*Man*] is not improperly conceived, when the former is traced back to reality, and the latter to ideality as their fundamental determination. Nature, however, is far from being so fixed and complete, as to subsist even without Spirit: in Spirit it first, as it were, attains its goal and its truth. And likewise, Spirit on its part is not merely an abstract other world of Nature, but it *is* only first true and proved as Spirit, as far as it contains Nature as transcended in itself (sect. 96, Z; quotation largely altered).

Hegel would be correct if he took the above on the level of the 'consistent naturalism or humanism' or 'species-life' detailed by Marx in the *Economic and philosophical manuscripts (1844)*.[36] In Marx's work 'man' develops 'his' nature through exploring the essence of objective nature (material cause) by *poiēsis* (formal cause).

However, Hegel's transition from the reality of 'determinate being' to the ideality of 'being-for-itself' does not express a humanisation of nature in history, as we see in Marx. Hegel leaps to the historical dimension without any mediation. What he defines abstractly as 'being-for-itself' implies modern alienation or the division of human species-life into physical and mental labour. In alienated life people mutually repulse each other in competition and nevertheless attract in exchange. Hegel expressed this implicitly in 'one and many'.

Marx translates 'repulsion and attraction' in the *Logic* into economic terms as competition among commodity-owners and their mutual dependency in commodity-exchange. How are competition and dependency mediated? This is not considered by Smith, who is satisfied with a view of money that lacks proof why and how labour becomes abstract, and whether or not there is any relationship between this abstraction and money.

By contrast, Hegel claims that the independent person brings about 'a simple form' with which 'he' transcends finite existence as an 'I' for 'we' and is thus organised as 'the superseded I', i.e. abstract intersubjective consciousness. Hegel is aware of the problem of the value-form or the genesis of money in his own logic of 'being-for-itself' or 'one and many'. But he does not develop this awareness into an analysis of the simplest form of value, the relation of one commodity to another, in which the commodity as subject expresses its own value in the use-value of another commodity.

Marx begins to analyse the form of value in the 'Chapter on Money' of the *Grundrisse*, obtaining his results by using Hegel's *Logic*. Hegel defines the special characteristic of 'spirit', which is distinguished from 'nature', as 'ideality'. The substance of this definition is specific to modern private property or value-consciousness, which the commodity-owner unconsciously objectifies in his product as exchange-value, and which the commodity-owner mistakenly assumes is inherent within it.

This value-consciousness is the alienated thought of the modern persons who form the exchange-relation. It is not a determination specific to the labour-process as such (natural formal cause) but a determination specific to persons in practical commodity-relations (alienated formal cause). Although Hegel does not explicitly define the 'ideality of being-for-itself' in that sense, he implies this substantive content.

By reading Hegel's definition of 'one and many' in that context, Marx applies it to his study of the value-form. He analyses the first form of value, where the value of one commodity is expressed in the use-value of another, as follows:

> A commodity is *exchange-value* only as far as it is expressed in another, i.e. as a relation [*Verhältnis*]. A bushel of wheat is worth so many bushels of rye; in this case wheat is exchange-value in as much as it is expressed in rye, and rye is exchange-value in as much as it is expressed in wheat (N 205, M 134; quotation partially altered).

In this citation Marx makes a clear distinction between the commodity as exchange-value and the commodity as equivalent. The owner of wheat in fact makes a value-thing (*ein Wertding*) of the wheat by expressing its value in rye. The owner speculates that wheat may be related to rye in this way, because wheat has an exchange-value in rye, or alternatively the owner speculates that the exchange-value is originally in the wheat itself. This speculation *de facto* abstracts exchange-value from the exchange-relation and mediates it. This thought (*Sache*) is one of value-abstraction, and the thought has a generality because it is ideal.

The wheat is related not only to rye, but to all commodities except itself, according to the specific abstraction made by its owner. It repulses and attracts other commodities as media for expressing its value. The value of one commodity is expressed in the use-values of many others. One commodity may be exchanged with many others, so it thus attains general exchangeability.

Here we see Marx's breakthrough in tackling the problem of the value-form. Because of the ideality and generality in the first value-form — the expression of the value of one commodity in the use-value of another — the first value-form necessarily leads to the second in Marx's analysis. In the second value-form, the value of one commodity is expressed in the use-values of many others. Hegel's 'being-for-itself' and 'one and many' reveal the logical character of the transition from the first value-form to the second, even though 'being-for-itself' in Hegel's *Logic* is not explicitly related to value. Reference to Hegel's *Logic* also shows us that Marx's presentation of the value-form in the *Grundrisse* is much closer to his final view, found in the second edition of *Capital*, than appears at first glance.

What takes place in the second form of the expression of value — the value of one commodity expressed in the use-values of many others? Each of the 'many' other commodities is also one 'one', and each has been used for the expression of value of one commodity. There are 'many ones'. The more these many other commodities take on the role of medium for the expression of value, the stronger their impulse to express their own value. Each of the 'many' also turns to 'one', with the same warrant to express its own value. This occurs in proportion to the maturity of the second form of value. These mutual claims to be the value-subject bring about the conversion of the second form to the third. In the third form commodities as 'many ones' express their values in the use-value of but one commodity, which they repulse and attract in common.

Marx defines the 'one' commodity as 'one general', in the following way:[37]

> It is posited as a *relation* [*Verhältnis*], more precisely as a relation in general [*allgemein*], not to one commodity but to every commodity, to every possible product. It expresses, therefore, a general relation [*ein allgemeines Verhältnis*]; the product which relates to itself as the realization of a *determinate quantum* [*ein bestimmtes Quantum*] of general labour, of social labour-time, and is therefore the equivalent of every other product in the proportion expressed in its exchange-value. Exchange-value presupposes social labour as the substance [*Substanz*] of all products, quite apart from their naturalness [*Natürlichkeit*]. Nothing can express a relation [*ein Verhältnis*] without relating to One [*zu Einem*], and there can be no general relation [*kein allgemeines Verhältnis*] unless it relates to one general thing [*zu einem Allgemeinen*] (N 205, M 133–4; quotation largely altered).

This conversion is defined as the transition from the second form of value to the third in *Capital*. In that context, as well as in *A contribution to the critique of political economy* of 1859, Marx says that the second form contains the third, which can be understood more easily with reference to Hegel's 'one and many', as interpreted above. In *A contribution to the critique of political economy* Marx writes as follows:

> Therefore the exchange-value of *this single commodity* [*diese einzelne Ware*] expresses itself exhaustively only in the infinitely many equations [*in den unendlich vielen Gleichungen*], where the use-values of all other commodities form their equivalent. Only in the sum of these equations or in the totality of different proportions where one commodity is exchangeable with any other commodity, and it is expressed exhaustively as *general equivalent*.[38]

Marx's study of the value-form in the 'Chapter on Money' is thus close to his final text when he explicates the transition from the second form of value to the third. However, his work in the 'Chapter on Money' has distinct limitations compared with the final version, because the value-form and the process of exchange are grasped as immediately related, so his analysis of the theoretical expression of value and the simultaneous realisation of exchange-value and use-value are not clearly separated in the *Grundrisse*. This is because he has not yet distinguished between value and exchange-value.[39]

Means of circulation and 'measure'

After analysing the value-form and its relation to the two types of circulation, Marx turns to money in its three determinations. He takes up his analysis with the second determination, money as means of circulation and realiser of prices:

> When we now go over the second determination [*Bestimmung*] of money, money as medium of exchange and realizer of prices, then we have found that in this case it must be present in a certain *quantity*; that the given weight of gold and silver which has been posited as a unit [*Einheit*] is required in a certain amount [*Anzahl*] in order to be adequate to this determination (N 208, M 136; quotation partially altered).

In the second determination of money 'this reality' (N 211, M 139), 'the material substance' (N 212, M 140) or 'material substratum' (ibid.) of money temporarily exists in the seller's hand, and soon vanishes (*verschwinden*) from it. The purpose of money in the first type of circulation $C_1-M-M-C_2$ is to exchange C_1 with C_2, or to obtain C_2 with C_1. Here money is 'a *semblance*, a fleeting mediation' (*ein Schein, verschwindende Vermittlung*) (N 210, M 138), acting to realise this purpose.

He confirms that the first determination of money (measure of value) and the second (means of circulation and realiser of prices) appear, for the present, independent of each other:

> . . . within the process [of circulation], as we have seen, the quantity, the amount of these objective symbols of the monetary unit is esential [in the second determination of money].

> Hence, while the material substance of money, its material substratum as a certain quantum of gold or silver, is indifferent within circulation, where money appears as something existing in opposition to commodities . . . it is there only a *symbol* for a certain amount of this unit; in its [first] determination as measure, however, where it was introduced only ideally, its material substratum was essential, but its quantity and even its existence as such were indifferent (N 212, M 140; quotation partially altered).

Those two determinations of money are analysed, using two facts, person (*Person*) and thing (*Sache*). In the first determination — measure of value — the person or commodity-owner is concerned with the existence or material substance of money (thing) as a purely theoretical entity (*in der Theorie* or *theoria*). However, in the second determination — means of circulation and realiser of prices — the person is indifferent in practice (*in der Praktik* or *praxis*) to the material substance of money, but interested instead in a certain nominal amount of money.

Monetary 'metallism' or realism and monetary nominalism are derived from the ideal representation of the real existence of money (money in its first determination as measure of value), and the practical realisation of imagined money in a certain amount of nominal money (money in its second determination as means of circulation and realiser of prices).

The metallist or realist speculates that money, which a person represents in the mind as an idea of value, exists in reality in the commodity, and realises itself in the practice of exchange; whereas the nominalist presumes that the value of money in circulation derives from a value that does not really exist in the commodity but is merely an idea in the minds of exchangers.

The two determinations of money are externally independent, an analytical phase based on 'measure' in Hegel's *Logic*:

> The identity between quality [= *the first determination*] and quantity [= *the second determination*], which is found in Measure, is at first only *implicit* [*an sich*], and not yet explicitly *posited*. In other words, each of these two determinations, the unification of which Measure is, likewise make themselves independent. On the one hand, the quantitative determinations of determinate being may be altered, without affecting its quality. On the other hand, this indifferent increase and

> decrease has its limit by exceeding which the quality is changed (sect. 108, Z; quotation largely altered).

Though Hegel gives an example of the change from water to steam or ice in the same section above, Marx continues to consider money in its two determinations:

> It is these contradictory determinations of money, [first] as measure, [and second] as realization of prices and as mere medium of exchange, which explains the otherwise inexplicable phenomenon that the *debasement* of metallic money, of gold, silver, through admixture of inferior metals, causes a depreciation of money and a rise in prices (N 212, M 140).

Here Marx is thinking of the dispute between John Locke and William Lowndes concerning the recoinage of silver.[40] Lowndes, the monetary nominalist, proposed a devaluation, i.e. renaming the old coins one shilling, even though they had been debased to four-fifths of their standard value in silver. His proposal was intended to settle the question of the real depreciation of silver coin with a merely nominal change. Locke, on the other hand, was a monetary realist or metallist, insisting on a restoration of the coinage, i.e. restoring the quantity of silver in the one shilling coin from its debased state to the old Elizabethan standard. He argued for a real adjustment in the coinage by increasing the amount of silver in it. Locke won the battle.

Marx took up the recoinage case in order to show that the two determinations of money are mutually influential. If the quality of material money as gold or silver decreases, its quantity as coinage increases.

Treasure and 'contradiction dissolves itself'

Marx then advances to the third determination:

> We now pass on to the third determination of money [treasure], which results from the second form of circulation: M–C–C–M; in which money appears not only as *medium* [second determination], nor as *measure* [first determination], but as an end-in-itself [third determination] (N 215, M 142; quotation partially altered).

Why does money appear as an end in itself? This is because the second type of circulation presents no qualitative difference at its end. At the beginning money is the same in its quality as at the end. The purpose of the second type of circulation, $M_1 - C - C - M_2$ is to obtain an M_2 greater than M_1, or to realise a surplus ($M_2 - M_1 = \Delta M$). Otherwise $M_2 < M_1$, and money decreases to zero, so the second form of circulation will cease to exist. Or if money is debased in quality, the same consequences will occur.

The purpose of the first type of circulation is individual consumption outside the economic process, whereas the purpose of the second type is an infinite movement, so money increases without qualitative change. Marx describes the third determination of money as follows:

> The *third determination* of money in its complete development presupposes the first two and is their unification. Money, therefore, has an independent existence outside circulation; it has stepped outside it. As a *particular* [*besondre*] commodity it can be transformed out of its form of money into that of luxury articles, gold and silver jewellery . . . or, as money, it can be *accumulated* to form a *treasure* [*Schatz*] (N 216, M 143; quotation partially altered).

Money is a specific form of community (*Gemeinwesen*). In bourgeois society, human abilities that derive from social relations are deformed into money. Money is not only a presupposition (*Voraus-Setzung*) but a resultant ('the posited') in the second form of circulation. Money changes everything into a commodity, including labour-power, because the products necessary for its reproduction are turned into commodities as alien property, which workers must buy with their money-wages:

> In order to function productively, money in its third determination, as we have seen, must be not only the presupposition but equally the result of circulation . . . It is inherent in the simple determination of money itself that it can exist as a developed moment of production only where [*wo*] *wage-labour* exists; that in this case, far from dissolving the social formation, it is rather a condition for its development and a driving-wheel for the development of all forces of production, material and spiritual (N 223, M 147–8; quotation partially altered).

As a consequence of wage-labour, 'the individual's industriousness has no limit' (N 224, M 148; quotation partially altered). The determination 'no limit' applied to wage-labour relates to its opposite pole, capital:

> Wherever it does not arise out of circulation — as in Spain — but has to be discovered corporeally, the nation is impoverished, whereas the nations which have to work in order to get it from the Spaniards develop the sources of wealth and really become rich (N 225, M 149; quotation partially altered).

In contrast to Spanish mercantilism, commercial capital in the Netherlands and England developed 'the sources of wealth' in their woollen industry. Commercial capital changed small-scale independent producers into wage-labourers through the putting-out system, even though these producers still appeared to be independent after the change. A large influx of gold and silver from the New World also caused real decreases in wages and rents, which benefited commercial capital even more. Commercial capital was thus originally accumulated capital, and it was transformed into industrial capital through manufacture.

In the *Grundrisse* Marx traces the path by which independent producers became industrial capitalists, and he argues that this was exceptional, without significance for his historical account.[41] His view of the transition from feudalism to capitalism changed, however, in the third manuscript version of *Capital*, dating from 1863–5,[42] although this change began during 1861–3, whilst he was writing the second manuscript version.[43]

Commercial capital seeks more money without limit. For that reason it forces immediate producers to work without limits, and they gradually become wage-labourers. Their forced wage-labour becomes 'measureless', an expression which comes from Hegel:

> *Measureless* [*das Masslose*] is, first of all, a quantitative excess of a qualitatively determined measure. However, this quantitative relation which lacks Measure, is still qualitative as well, so Measureless is also a measure. These two transitions, from quality to quantum and from quantum to quality, can be represented as *an infinite progress* — as the abrogation and restoration of measure in Measureless (sect. 109, quotation largely altered).[44]

In the transition from 'quality' to 'quantum', Marx traces the first determination of money (measure of value) in its transition to the second (means of circulation). In the transition from 'quantum' to 'another quality', he traces the third determination (treasure) as a unification of the first and second. Money in its third determination is surplus-money removed from circulation. How are the first and second determinations unified in the third? Marx writes as follows:

> Money . . . in the form in which it independently steps outside of and against circulation, is the negation (negative unity) [*die Negation (negative Einheit)*] of its determination as medium of circulation and measure (N 228, M 152).

Why are they negatively unified? This is because they subsist through mutual negation. Money in one determination is negated by money in its other determinations, as follows:

1. Money as measure of value (first determination) negates money as means of circulation (second determination), because the first is qualitative and the second quantitative.
2. Money as measure of value (first determination) negates money as a means for realising prices (second determination), because the first is qualitative and the second quantitative.
3. Money as measure of value (first determination) is negated by money as means of circulation (second determination), because the second is quantitative and the first qualitative.
4. Money as measure of value (first determination) is further negated by money as surplus-money (third determination), because the third is quantitative and the first qualitative.

Marx writes:

> As money in this third determination, the amount of itself as of a definite material quantum is essential. If its quality as general wealth is given, then there is no difference within it, other than the quantitative. It represents a greater or lesser amount of general wealth, depending on whether it possesses a given quantum of the general wealth in a greater or lesser amount (N 229, M 153; quotation largely altered).

Therefore money seeks more money with a standard quality, and is measureless. How can we see that historically? Commercial capitalists gathered together producers who became only nominally independent, and were in fact transformed into wage-labourers in manufacture. Corresponding to that change, commercial capitalists were transformed into industrial capitalists, and that resulted in the transition from mercantilism to industrial capitalism.

Presupposing this historical transition, Marx looks for the beginning of the logical transition from money to capital, and he finds it in the third determination of money, treasure. He accomplishes this by using Hegel's conception 'contradiction dissolves itself'.

As we have just noted, money in the third determination is the negative unity of the first and second determinations, in which each determination is negated by its opposite: 'Money in its final, completed determination now appears in all aspects as a contradiction, which dissolves itself, and drives towards its own dissolution' (N 233, M 157; quotation partially altered).

Either in its first or in its second determination, money negates money in its opposing determinations by a process of self-determination. In other words, each determination attains self-affirmation through the negation of its opposite, which negates it, so it negates its own negation. Therefore the determination 'quality' (the first determination) is the negation of its opposite 'quantity', i.e. the negation of 'quality', so in short, the determination 'quality' is equivalent to the negation of its own negation, 'quantity'.

In the same way and in the same sense, the determination 'quantity' negates its opposite determination 'quality', i.e. the negation of 'quantity'. Thus the determination 'quantity' is equivalent to the negation of its own negation, 'quality'. Each of the two determinations is a determination or affirmation mediated through the negation of the negation. Marx's quotation of Spinoza's thesis that 'determination is negation' (*determinatio est negatio*) (N 90, M 27) is utilised in his analyses of the negative unity of the first two determinations of money.

'Quality' now persists through mediation, or the negation of the negation, and is not self-subsistent. It is not a fixed particular quality, but the abstract quality or the generality which mediates and maintains itself through as many concrete sorts of quality as possible. 'Quantity' is now also mediated. It is not a fixed quantum in a particular quality, but a variable quantity, indeed a quantity increasing through metamorphoses.

Marx analyses money in its third determination as treasure in accordance with Hegel's description of the transition from 'being' to 'essence' in the last section of the 'Minor Logic':

> The Infinity, the affirmation as negation of the negation [*die Affirmation als Negation der Negation*] now has its aspects in Quality and Quantity, instead of the more abstract aspects of Being and Nothing or Something and Other. These aspects *a.* have in the first place *transited* [*übergegangen*] from quality to quantity (sect. 98), and from quantity to quality (sect. 105), and thus are both shown up as *negations* [*Negationen*]. *b.* But in their *unity* (in measure [*dem Masse*]) they are first of all distinct, and the one is only *by means of* [*vermittels*] the other. And *c.* after the immediacy of this unity has turned out to be self-annulling, this unity is now *posited* as what is *implicit* [*an sich*], as simple relation-to-itself, which contains Being-in-general and those forms that are annulled in it. — Being or immediacy, which is mediation *with itself* and relation to itself through negation of itself, and which is consequently likewise a mediation which annuls itself into relation to itself, or into immediacy, is *Essence* [*das Wesen*] (sect. 111; quotation largely altered).[45]

Marx grasps the third determination of money as an 'affirmation as negation of the negation'. Money in the third determination is doubly mediated by the first and second determinations.

Firstly, money in the third determination does not now merely measure the value of a commodity, but is transformed into a value which subsists through a ceaseless transition from one form to another.

Secondly, value is no longer a nominal, fixed quantum but a variable quantum, an increasing quantity.

Therefore money in its third determination is no longer simple money but implicitly a form of capital. Correspondingly value-consciousness now implies a consciousness of increasing value or a capitalist consciousness.

Marx finds these implications of capital in value itself by using Hegel's definition of 'essence' as 'being and immediacy', which is 'mediation *with itself* and relation to itself through negation of itself'. Marx concludes his discussion in the 'Chapter on Money' as follows:

> With circulation, the *determined* price is presupposed, and circulation as money posits it only formally. The *determinateness* of exchange-value itself, or the measure [*das Mass*] of price, must now itself appear as an act of circulation. Posited in this way, exchange-value is *capital* [*das Kapital*], and circulation is posited at the same time as an act of production (N 235, M 158).

In the first, simple type of circulation $C_1 - M - M - C_2$, the owner of commodity C_1 determines its price. This price, determined ideally, is realised in money, which is used to purchase another commodity C_2. Therefore in simple circulation, price or exchange-value is not as such the purpose of the activity, but a mere temporary form which mediates a material transition from C_1 to C_2. However, in the third determination of money as treasure, money has another potential mission. It accomplishes this in an act of circulation, the purpose of which is an increase of exchange-value itself as value is measured and prices realised. That second type of circulation is capital. Since capital is an expanding value-relation in which exchange is carried out in terms of equivalent values, capital cannot subsist merely by 'an act of circulation'. It must be mediated through 'an act of production', in which it extracts surplus-labour and realises it as surplus-value in circulation. In that way capital can persist.

As previously noted, Marx grasps money in its third determination as a negative unity or 'a contradiction which dissolves itself', a reference to Hegel, who wrote that contradiction dissolves itself into 'ground':

> This contradictory side of course dissolves itself into nothing, it withdraws into its negative unity. Now the thing [*das Ding*], the subject, the Notion, is just this negative unity itself; it is inherently self-contradictory, but it is no less the *dissolved contradiction* [*der aufgelöste Widerspruch*]: it is the *ground* [*der Grund*] that contains and supports its determinations.[46]

Marx grasps the contradiction of money as follows. The contradiction of money as 'negative unity' dissolves itself when money saved from circulation as treasure returns to circulation in order to transform the conditions of production as the 'ground' of exchange-value. Marx develops this insight at the beginning of the 'Chapter on Capital' in the *Grundrisse*.

3
The 'Chapter on Capital' and the Doctrine of Essence, Part One: 'Generality of Capital'

The transition from money to capital and 'positing reflection'

At the beginning of the 'Chapter on Capital' in the *Grundrisse* (N 250, M 173),[1] Marx defines a new, fourth determination of money, 'money as capital', distinguishing it from the third determination — 'treasure' or 'money as money' or 'money as an end in itself'. Then he considers the relation between value and capital as they were developed in theory and in history:

> As in theory [*in der Theorie*] the notion [*Begriff*] of value precedes that of capital, but on the other hand pre-posits [*voraus-setzen*] a mode of production grounded on capital, for its pure development, so the same thing takes place in practice [*in der Praxis*] . . . The existence of value in its purity and generality pre-posits a mode of production in which the individual product has ceased to exist for the producer in general and even more for the individual labourer, and where nothing exists unless it is realized through circulation . . . This determination of value, then, pre-posits a given historic stage of the mode of social production and it is something given with that mode, hence, a historic relation.
>
> At the same time, individual moments of the determinations of value develop in the earlier stages of the historic process of social production and appear as its result.
>
> Hence, within the system of bourgeois society, capital follows immediately after money.
>
> *In history* [*in der Geschichte*], *other systems come before* [*bourgeois*

> *society*], and they form the material basis of a still incomplete development of value (N 251–2, M 174–5; quotation partially altered).

In theoretical order, value precedes capital, and 'capital follows immediately after money'. In other words, money, which has developed from commodity-relationships, advances to capital, and capital structures material production and posits the circulation of commodities. This forms a circular process — logical presupposition (*Voraus-Setzung*), then positing (*Setzung*), which becomes the next presupposition.

However, in order for money to become capital, the following four conditions must be presupposed (*voraus-gesetzt*):

1. Free exchange must have become widespread throughout society (*Gemeinwesen*).
2. Most of the funds for production and consumption must have become free funds.
3. Because of the transformation of the funds for consumption into commodities, most of the immediate producers must have become wage-labourers and most labour-power must have become a commodity.[2]
4. Money must have been accumulated to such an extent that capital will have been formed.

When Marx writes that capital follows immediately (*unmittelbar*) after money, he is presupposing that the four logical conditions listed above are extant in bourgeois society. These four conditions have been posited in actual fact by commercial capital in the course of history and have become presuppositions (*Voraus-Setzungen*) for the transformation of money into capital. It remains to be demonstrated how commercial capital then posits the presuppositions for the development of industrial capital in the course of history. Once that is done, Marx can write that capital follows immediately after money, though he later appends to this logical transformation a discussion of the economic formations which precede capitalist production, a section of the *Grundrisse* known as 'Pre-capitalist economic formations' (N 459–515, M 367–417).[3]

When the four logical conditions are established in reality, money has then matured in its three determinations — measure of value, means of circulation, treasure or surplus-money. It has an impulse to complete the transformation into capital because labour-power, not simply its product, has become a commodity.

In his analysis Marx takes on the logical transformation of money into capital, before he considers the historical conditions for that transformation. Presupposing those historical conditions — the destruction of the primitive community and the process of primitive accumulation of capital — he develops or posits the logical transformation of money into capital. That development consists in the process of production of surplus-value and the accumulation of capital. Then, with those theoretical demonstrations as criteria, he searches for the development of the four historical conditions listed above which clarify his account of the logical development of capital. The order of analysis for capital that Marx uses in the *Grundrisse* is the logico-historical order previously employed in the *Economic and philosophical manuscripts (1844)*,[4] then used again in *Capital*.

In the *Grundrisse* Marx explores the general formation of a social system in history:

> It must be kept in mind that the new productive forces and relations of production do not develop out of *nothing* [*Nichts*], nor drop from the sky, nor from the womb of the self-positing Idea [*die sich selbst setzende Idee*]; but from within and in opposition to the existing development of production and the inherited, traditional relations of property. While in the completed bourgeois system every economic relation preposits [*voraus-setzen*] every other in its bourgeois economic form, and everything posited [*jedes Gesetzte*] is thus also a presupposition [*Voraus-Setzung*], this is the case with every organic system. This organic system itself, as a totality, has its presuppositions, and its development to its totality consists precisely in subordinating all elements of society to itself, or in creating out of it the organs which it still lacks. The organic system historically becomes a totality. The process of becoming this totality forms a moment of its process of coming-to-be, of its development (N 278, M 201; quotation largely altered).

In the quotation cited above, Marx reflects on Hegel's logic of 'positing reflection'. Hegel writes, '*Positing* Reflection begins from Nothing [*Nichts*]',[5] and Marx criticises this conception, arguing that the bourgeois economic system has developed neither from 'the self-positing idea' nor from 'nothing'. Hegel also comments that 'the positing has no presupposition',[6] and Marx uses this idea constructively in his critique.

Once the bourgeois economic system is established or posited, capital posits the presuppositions (*Voraus-Setzungen*) of its continued existence as results of the activity of capital itself. Therefore what is posited (*das Gesetzte*) is the same as what is presupposed (*vorausgesetzt*). This order — from presupposition to positing (*Setzung*) to what is posited or is a resultant — forms a circulation. In that way the self-reproduction of the bourgeois economy shares a circular logic with Hegel's 'positing reflection'. They are the same so long as they mediate their presuppositions within themselves. Through that mediation, their existence is determined through self-reproduction. Presupposition and 'the posited' are given their identities in this circulation, and 'identity' is the simplest determination of 'essence'. This self-identity is analogous to self-reproduction in the bourgeois economy.

Hegel asserts that 'positing reflection' has no presupposition, suggesting that what precedes presupposition is identical with what it posits. However, with respect to the bourgeois economic system, the very presuppositions of its existence were originally posited in the historical process by which pre-capitalist forms of society were destroyed, and it was from those elements that bourgeois society was built up. Far from having no presuppositions, the bourgeois economy has historical presuppositions derived directly from the past. The logical presuppositions of the self-reproduction of the bourgeois economic system are posited in history, and are independent of the logical presuppositions identified by Marx.

At the beginning of the 'Chapter on Capital' in the *Grundrisse*, Marx confirms this methodology. When he presupposes conditions for the transformation of money into capital, he follows the movement of capital to the stage of accumulation, and then traces how the conditions were developed in the historical process by which primitive accumulation occurred and the primitive community was destroyed. After that confirmation, he brings his analysis of the bourgeois economic system into focus: 'But we are dealing here with developed bourgeois society, which is already moving on its own foundation' (N 253, M 175).

On that basis he presents the following problem, later formulated as the 'Rhodus problem' in *Capital*:

> 1. Capital comes initially from circulation, and, moveover, its point of departure is money (N 253, M 175).

> 2. On the other side it is equally clear that the simple movement of exchange-values, such as is present in pure circulation, can never realize capital (N 254, M 176).

This is the 'Rhodus problem': the transformation of money into capital must be realised both within and outside the process of circulation. In Marx's words, 'These are the conditions of the problem. *Hic Rhodus, hic salta!*'.[7]

In a passage in the *Grundrisse* that occurs just after point 2 above, Marx refers again to the contradiction within money resolving itself: 'As soon as money steps back into circulation, it dissolves itself in a series of exchange-processes with commodities which are consumed, hence it is lost as soon as its purchasing power is exhausted' (N 254, M 176; quotation partially altered).

These two problems — the 'Rhodus problem' and the contradiction within money — are the same, and they both exist in the sphere of circulation, quite apart from production. The conditions for the transformation of money into capital cannot be met entirely in circulation. When money returns to circulation, it meets the 'Rhodus problem', i.e. how to generate a surplus for capital-accumulation when only equivalents are exchanged. Money must be transformed into the conditions of production in order to solve the problem:

> *Circulation therefore does not carry within itself the principle of self-renewal. The movements of the latter are pre-posited* [*voraus-gesetzt*] *to it*, not posited by it . . . Its immediate being is therefore pure semblance. *It is the phenomenon* [*Phänomen*] *of a process taking place behind it* (N 254–5, M 177; quotation partially altered).

In a passage strikingly like the one by Marx quoted above, Hegel writes: 'It [*Immediacy*] is mere *Unessence* [*Unwesen*], or *Semblance* [*Schein*].'[8] 'Semblance in Essence is not the Semblance of an Other, but *Semblance in itself, Semblance of Essence itself*'.[9]

Marx thinks that commodities and money in simple circulation are results of the 'principle of self-renewal' or reproduction, and that at first they appear independently as 'immediacies' not mediated by anything. That appearance, however, is a mere semblance of the truth. Money must return to circulation, not to remain there, but to change into conditions for production. In that way Marx traces the path of value in a process that moves from non-circulation to circulation and thence to production.

In short, the contradiction in money in its third determination — money as 'treasure' or 'surplus-money' — dissolves itself into the 'ground' of production. That logical order — from contradiction to 'ground' — is based on Hegel's *Logic*: '*Contradiction dissolves itself*.'[10] 'The dissolved contradiction is therefore ground [*Grund*].'[11]

Marx traces the movement by which value, in order to increase, must advance from non-circulation to circulation and thence to production. And he connects this process with the logic that 'contradiction dissolves itself' into 'ground':

> While, originally, the act of social production appeared as the positing of exchange-values and this, in its later development, as circulation — as completely developed reciprocal movement of exchange-values — now, circulation itself returns back into the activity which posits or produces exchange-values. It returns into it as into its ground [*Sie geht darein zurück als in ihren Grund*] (N 255, M 177).

Money transforms itself into the conditions for production and then returns to the point where exchange-values in the form of commodities and money have been produced or posited. At the beginning of the 'Chapter on Capital', Marx refers to Hegel's 'positing reflection' or circular logic that moves from presupposition (*Voraus-Setzung*) to positing (*Setzung*). But he does so on the basis of his own presupposition that the four conditions for the transition of money into capital have already been established in the course of history. The transition from contradiction to 'ground' at the beginning of Hegel's Doctrine of Essence is related by Marx to the movement of 'money as capital' from non-circulation to circulation and thence to production, in order to resolve the contradiction between 'money as capital' and the 'quantitative barrier' (*Schranke*) it must cross between equivalence and increase or surplus (N 270, M 194).

The exchange between capital and labour, the labour-process and the valorisation-process, and 'form, substance, matter and content'

In tracing the movement of 'money as capital' from circulation to production, Marx applies Hegel's dictum in logic that contradiction dissolves itself into 'ground'. 'Money as capital' transforms itself into conditions for production (productive labour and the means of production), and thus returns from circulation to production, which corresponds to 'ground' in the Doctrine of Essence.[12]

In order to investigate the further connections between Marx's *Grundrisse* and Hegel's *Logic*, we must note that Hegel describes a complex subsumption of substance, matter and content under the concept 'form' as follows:

> Form at first stands opposed to Essence [*Wesen* = Substance],[13] and is then Ground-relation in general, and its determinations are the Ground and Grounded. It further stands opposed to Matter [*Materie*], and then is Determining Reflection, and its determinations are Determination of Reflection itself and its persistence. Finally it stands opposed to Content [*Inhalt*], where its determinations again are itself and Matter. What before was the self-identical first Ground, then persistence in general, and lastly Matter — passes beneath the domination of Form [*Herrschaft der Form*] and is once more one of its determinations.[14]

Hegel argues that 'form' subsumes 'essence' or 'substance', 'matter' and 'content' concomitantly under itself. By contrast Marx rearranges those four categories into three pairs:

1. form and substance;
2. form and content;
3. form and matter.

Marx has already analysed the economic implications of 'form and substance' in the 'Chapter on Money'. He explicates the economic significance of 'form and content' in the exchange between capital and labour, and that of 'form and matter' in his consideration of the labour-process.

As we have seen in our analysis of the 'Chapter on Money', 'labour in general' is unconsciously abstracted in commodity-relations as a 'social substance': 'The substance [*Substanz*] of value is not at all the particular natural substance [*die besondre natürliche Substanz*], but rather objectified labour [*die vergegenständlichte Arbeit*]' (N 299, M 219). Owners of labour-products equate them with each other as value in private exchange, and through that equation, each concrete form of labour is abstracted as objectified labour, a social substance, which grounds and regulates value. Exchangers presume that they equate their products with each other as values, because as values they appear to be equivalents. Thus the unconscious acts of exchangers are reflected in a perverse way in their consciousness. What seems to them to be value is only an ideal expression of their relation within private exchange. That relation, which is posited as they equate their products, is alienated from them as value. Marx later calls this alienated relation a 'form' or 'value-form' in *Capital*.

In the *Grundrisse* Marx just touches on the analysis of the value-form, but does not as yet develop it from its first to its fourth and final form as coins and currency. Rather he begins the study of value, using the term 'substance' in two ways: 'natural substance' in the sense of use-value, and 'social substance' in the sense of abstract labour. The reason why he adopts the word 'substance' in those two senses is that he understands social substance as something mediated with or materialised in a natural substance. The terms 'natural substance' and 'social substance' are an adaptation of Aristotle's concepts 'primary substance' and 'secondary substance'. Marx equates primary substance with natural substance, and secondary substance with social substance.

However, form and substance are not yet paired in the *Grundrisse*, as they are in the later theory of the value-form in *Capital*, because in the *Grundrisse* Marx has not yet distinguished value from exchange-value. He uses the word 'relation' in the sense of 'value-form' (N 143, M 77–8), and therefore it is possible to say that he in fact uses the pair 'form and substance' in the *Grundrisse*.

Marx understands what Hegel calls ideality of 'being-for-itself' as the logical expression of the alienated relation of exchange or 'form' as value. He sees the alienated relation or value-form in 'being-for-itself'. 'Form' or relation and social substance are historical *par excellence* in the *Grundrisse*, where he connects them with the exchange of commodities. 'Form' and 'substance' are determinations of commodity-exchange, considered abstractly. 'Form' is what becomes alienated and independent from the people who exchange commodities, and 'substance' is what grounds and regulates 'form', because it is abstracted from concrete labour when commodities are equated as values.

This pair 'form and substance' is connected with the next pair, 'form and content'.[15] The alienated relation or 'form' becomes separated (*chōriston*) as value and materialised as money through the unconscious acts of commodity-owners. Value is transubstantiated (N 308, M 228) into another natural substance, gold or silver, so the contradiction between use-value and value develops into an exterior opposition between commodities and money.

'Form' and 'content' are determinations of the commodity and money in exchange-relations. Money is 'form', which has value as its main component and use-value as a subordinate component, whereas the commodity is 'content', which has, by contrast, use-value as its main component and value as a subordinate one.

Marx then makes a distinction between two ways in which money as 'form' and the commodity as 'content' are related. He does this in connection with the two types of circulation: C–M–M–C and M–C–C–M. The first way is the determination of 'form and content' in the case of simple circulation C_1–M–M–C_2, which is composed of two kinds of exchange, first selling (C_1–M) and then buying (M–C_2). The second way is the determination of money and commodity in the exchange between capital and labour, which the second type of circulation reflects. In its full expression it is M–C($L_p + P_m$) . . . P . . . C′–M′, where L_p = 'labour-power' (or in the *Grundrisse* 'labour-ability') and P_m = 'means of production'.

Marx describes simple circulation, through which individuals obtain the means of consumption, as follows:

> . . . money for the commodity: i.e. the exchange-value of the commodity disappears [*verschwinden*] in exchange for its material content [*ihr materielle Inhalt*]; or commodity for money, i.e. its content [*Inhalt*] disappears in exchange for its form [*Form*] as exchange-value. In the first case, the form of exchange-value is extinguished; in the second, its substance [= content]; in both, therefore, its realization is its disappearance (N 260, M 184; quotation partially altered).

In simple circulation a content obtained through exchange becomes a use-value or object for individual consumption, and the form of exchange is the simple one in which exchange is terminated, whether it is an equivalent exchange or not. That 'form' disappears after mediating the 'content' of exchange. Therefore that 'form' does not subsist by itself, but mediates itself with 'content' of various kinds. In that way 'an actual relation of exchange-value and use-value' (N 269, M 193; quotation largely altered) does not occur, as it does in the second type of circulation.

In the second type of circulation, the exchange between capital and labour is different with respect to 'form' and 'content':

> This [= the simple exchange] concerns only the *form* [*Form*] of the exchange; but does not form its content [*Inhalt*]. In the exchange of capital for labour, *value* is not a measure for the exchange of two use-values, but is rather the *content* [*Inhalt*] *of the exchange* itself (N 469, M 376–7).

The exchange between capital and labour is the same as a simple exchange from the point of view of the wage-labourer, because wage-labourers sell their commodity, labour-power (C_1) for money and then buy commodities which form the means for individual consumption (C_2). However, from the standpoint of the capitalist, things are different. For the capitalist, the use-value of labour-power is the use-value unique to itself, 'use-value for *value*' (N 469, M 376), a possibility for positing value and surplus-value. In the second type of circulation 'value is . . . the content, and this form [is] *value*' (N 272, M 196). Therefore the 'form' of exchange becomes its 'content'. The 'content' of the exchange between capitalist and labourer, from the standpoint of the capitalist, is 'form as content'.[16] This is a 'form' which persists as its own 'content', or which becomes its own 'content', through a mediation of itself with various 'contents' that are natural substances or use-values. In that way the real relation between exchange-value and use-value is developed.

Presupposing the existence of the means of production as 'the content of capital' (*Inhalt des Kapitals*), Marx expresses the immediate results of the exchange between capital and labour. This 'content' of capital is distinguished from its 'formal relation' (*Formbeziehung*) (N 302, M 221). The 'content' of capital includes the elements of the 'process of production in general' (N 303, M 223), and the relation between 'matter' (*Materie*) or raw material and instrument, and 'form' or labour (N 302, M 221). This is not the 'form as content' of the exchange between capital and labour. Rather these elements in the 'content' of capital are factors of the labour-process (N 304 f., M 223 f.).

Marx then considers capital's own 'formal relation' to its elements (N 302, M 222), both in the valorisation process and in the process of production of relative surplus-value. After that, in his consideration of the twofold character of labour — labour as creator of new value and preserver of old values — he takes up the relation between the 'content' of capital and its 'form'.

In the valorisation process Marx traces the realisation of 'form as content'. In that process labour-power represents the possibility (*Möglichkeit*) of valorisation, but this is a simple or abstract possibility. It becomes actual in connection with the means of production and consumption, and it realises 'form as content' when invested as capital. Surplus-value or 'form' is thus posited through the consumption of labour-power.

In considering the valorisation process Marx brings into focus one aspect of the realisation of 'form as content' or increasing value. When considering relative surplus-value, he includes moments of use-value or 'content' as means of subsistence for the labourer. 'Content' as use-value is thus mediated with 'form' as surplus-value. If the quantity of labour objectified in a certain amount of the means of individual consumption or 'content' decreases, because productivity has increased, then surplus-value or 'form' increases proportionately.

In the twofold character of labour — labour as creator of new value and preserver of old values — another moment of the value or 'form' of the means of production is introduced. Living or concrete labour is subsumed under the process of production of capital in order to produce new use-value or content. At the same time the value or 'form' of the means of production is transferred and preserved through the consumption of old concrete use-values or 'content' in the means of production.

There are three sorts of use-value related to the production of the commodity as capital — the use-value of labour-power, the use-value of the means of life for the labourer, and the use-value of the means of production. They are mediated in a complex way in the product as commodity-capital (C + V + S), and they are introduced one by one as determinate moments of the valorisation process, the process of producing relative surplus-value, and the twofold character of labour.

'Form as content' is a mere potential within the negative unity of money in its third determination, treasure or 'money as money', but 'form as content' actually emerges in the exchange of 'money as capital' for labour. It realises itself through mediation of the three sorts of use-value listed above, making a complex structure of 'form and content' in the labour-product as capital. Each 'content' or use-value of capital is converted (*umschlagen*) through mediation into its own 'form' or value. The conversion occurs in the accumulation of capital, considered below.

Let us advance to 'form and matter'. As cited in the Preface to this book, Alfred Schmidt has called his readers' attention to this pair of concepts. This pair has its origin in the work of Aristotle, and Hegel has adapted them from Aristotle as 'ground' in his *Logic*.

Aristotle defines 'form' and 'matter' as causes of a product in the following way: a producer imagines what and how to produce, using his mental abilities (*telos, causa finalis*, final cause) before actual production takes place. The producer realises this image by using his physical ability (*archē, causa efficiens*, efficient cause), and making use of materials (*hylē, causa materialis*, material cause) that exist outside himself (*eidos, causa formalis*, formal cause).

Hegel develops Aristotle's four causes (*eidos, telos, archē* and *hylē*) into other concepts under 'actuality' (*Wirklichkeit*) in the *Logic*, changing *telos* to 'concern' or 'thing' (*Sache*), *archē* to 'activity' (*Tätigkeit*) and *hylē* to 'condition' (*Bedingung*) (sect. 148).

On what level does Marx appropriate Hegel's interpretation of Aristotle? First of all, he interprets it on a trans-historical level as three factors of the process of production in general or the labour process. He interprets what Hegel calls 'concern' and 'activity', both of which are 'forms', as mental and physical factors of labour-power, and he interprets 'condition' as 'matter' or means of production:

> . . . in connection with labour as activity [*Tätigkeit*], the matter [*Stoff*], the objectified labour, has only two relations, that of the *raw material*, i.e. of the formless [*formlos*] matter, the mere matter for the form-positing [*Formsetzend*], purposive activity of labour, and that of the *instrument of labour*, the objective means which subjective activity inserts between itself and an object, as its conductor (N 298–9, M 219).

'Form' and 'substance' are historical determinations in private exchange, whereas 'form' and 'matter' are trans-historical determinations in the labour-process. How are the two pairs then connected with each other? Marx analyses the connection between them in the following way: 'form' or value, which has been grounded on social substance and mediated with natural substance, is now separated from a non-specific natural substance and transubstantiated into a specific natural substance such as gold or silver as the 'money-subject' (N 167, M 99, etc.). This substance is in fact 'money as capital'. 'Money as capital' or 'form' is then linked to the conditions of production or 'content' which is analysed at first from a trans-historical standpoint. In that analysis it appears as the relation between 'form' and 'matter'. 'Form and substance' and 'form and matter' are thus mediated and linked together:

> Now . . . in the process of production, capital distinguishes itself as form [*Form*] from itself as [*natural*] substance [*Substanz*]. It is both aspects at once, and at the same time the relation of both to one another. But . . . it still only appeared as this relation *in itself* [*an sich*]. The relation is not *posited* yet, or it is posited initially only in the determination of one of its two moments, the *material* moment, which divides internally as matter [*Materie*] (raw material and instrument) and form [*Form*] (labour), and, which, as a relation between both of them, as an actual process, is itself only a material relation again — a relation of the two material elements which form the content of capital [*Inhalt des Kapitals*] as distinct from its formal relation as capital [*Formbeziehung als Kapital*] (N 301–2, M 221).

Marx then considers labour-power and the means of production. These are structured by money-capital into a 'material relation', 'the content of capital as distinct from its formal relation as capital' or 'form and matter'. Using the two terms, derived originally from Aristotle, Marx refers to the subjective moment of the labour-process as 'form', and to the objective moments as 'matter', and then to the relation between the two kinds of moment as a 'material relation'.

Using these definitions Marx clarifies the twofold relation between 'form' and 'matter'. Man is 'form' (*eidos*) in relation to nature as 'matter' (*hylē*). This 'form' (*eidos*) is analysed into *telos* (final cause) and *archē* (efficient cause). The final cause is the human mind, and the efficient cause is the human body. The human mind and body are themselves defined as *eidos* and *hylē*, showing the superiority of mind over body, so human nature subsists because mind rules body in the way that 'man' as 'form' (*eidos*) rules nature as 'matter' (*hylē*). Therefore:

1. The human mind (*telos*) is '*eidos* as *eidos*' (*eidos* as such).
2. The human body is *archē* as *hylē* in its determinate relation to the human mind (*telos*); but:
3. So long as human beings change given forms of nature (*hylē*)

into new ones that are determined by the human mind (*eidos* as such), the human body is '*archē* as *eidos*' in relation to nature, and:

4. Nature is '*hylē* as *hylē*' (*hylē* as such).[17]

By analysing the complex relation presented above, Marx demonstrates how these four factors are organised in capitalist production.

For Marx it is capitalist private property that divides the natural unity of 'man' and nature, and divides the immediate unity of human beings in society. Because of the capitalist expropriation of nature (*hylē* as such) — that is, land and products of labour — the capitalist monopolises the human mind (*telos* or '*eidos* as *eidos*'). By contrast, wage-labourers exist as such, because they are alienated from nature by the capitalist, and the wage-labourer must also alienate labour-power, confining it to the human body (rather than including the mind) and to its productive relationship with nature, because the wage-labourer must subordinate labour to the capitalist. In capitalism the human being as 'form' appears to be dependent on nature as 'matter', the inverse of the wage-labourer's real dependency on the capitalist.

The capitalist is engaged as human mind (*telos* or *eidos*) in this role, alienating natural physical ability — the body's productive relationship with nature — to the wage-labourer. The proper activity of the capitalist consists in measuring, maintaining and increasing value, and therefore capitalist activity is different from natural *telos*. The capitalist's *telos* is limited to structuring value-relations, and the capitalist identifies the metamorphoses of capital with the value-relations that are dealt with abstractly in the mind, so the capitalist 'obtains this ideal determination' of capital (*seine ideal Bestimmung erhalten*) (N 298, M 218). When a distinction is made between the capitalist and the conditions of production, the former appears as the personification of capital and the latter as a 'material relation'. Wage-labour appears as '*archē* as *hylē*', means of production as '*hylē* as *hylē*', and both appear as *hylē* against the capitalist, who appears as *eidos par excellence*.

However, this represents an external distinction between formal and material moments. Later on they are mediated within the process of capitalist production in which the four factors mentioned above are rearranged.

First, the wage-labourer does not appear as *eidos* in the labour-process, but as '*archē* as *hylē*' to the capitalist, and as '*archē* as *eidos*' or as agent to the means of production, which appears as '*hylē* as *hylē*'. The wage-labourer acts as a twofold *archē*.

Secondly, living labour subsumed under capitalist production has a twofold character. Here Marx is successful for the first time in analysing it. Labour not only adds new value (V + M), but preserves and transfers old value (C) from the means of production.

The twofold character of labour and its twofold *archē* are related in the following ways. Firstly, the *archē* of the labourer works as a 'natural *eidos*' and produces a new product ('*hylē* as *hylē*'), and preserves the 'natural substance' of the means of production ('*hylē* as such') in a 'substance with another form' (N 312, M 230). At the same time as an agent for the capitalist (*eidos* as such), the *archē* of the labourer ('*archē* as *eidos*') objectifies new value (V + S) and preserves old value already objectified in the means of production (C) through the consumption of its own use-value. It acts as 'the mediating activity through which capital *valorizes* itself' (N 305, M 225; quotation partially altered) in relation to the means of production (*hylē* as such). It reproduces value (V), increases value (S) and preserves 'social substance' as constant capital (C). The twofold character of labour or *archē* is the actuality through which the 'content' of capital (which includes the use-value of labour-power and of the means of production) converts itself into the 'form' of capital, i.e. the value of capital as a product.[18]

Labour-power as general substance and 'relation of substantiality'

Capital can persist because it subsumes labour as 'general substance' (*die allgemeine Substanz*), so Marx now considers labour-power (*Arbeitsvermögen*) as general substance. Through the subsumption of labour-power, capital maintains its existence:

> Capital is, by its notion, money, but not merely money in the simple form of gold and silver, nor merely as money in opposition to circulation, but in the form of all substances — commodities . . . The communal substance of all commodities, i.e. their substance not as material stuff, as physical determination, but their communal substance as *commodities* and hence *exchange-value*, is this, that they are *objectified labour*. The only thing distinct from *objectified* labour is *non-objectified* labour, labour which is still objectifying itself, *labour* as subjectivity . . . The only *use-value*, therefore, which can form the opposite pole is *labour* (N 271–2, M 195–6; quotation partially altered).

> . . . the use-value which he [the labourer] offers, exists only as capacity, ability [*Fähigkeit*, *Vermögen*] of his bodily existence; has no existence [*Dasein*] apart from that. The objectified labour, which is necessary not only to maintain the general substance [*die allgemeine Substanz*] on which his labour-power [*Arbeitsvermögen*] exists, i.e. to maintain the labourer himself bodily, but also to modify [*modifizieren*] this general substance to develop its particular ability, is the labour objectified in it (N 282–3, M 205; quotation partially altered).

What does the 'general substance' mentioned above actually mean? In general, capital depends on labour-power. But why is it referred to as 'general substance'? Here Marx contrasts 'general' with 'particular'. The labourer consumes particular substances as the means for individual consumption and is engaged in a particular job. The labourer is a particular substance as labour with respect to capital, and the labourer produces a particular substance or product using particular substances as means of production. So far the connection between various kinds of particular substances appears merely as a relation between the capitalist and labourers as individuals.

However, the labourer must engage in various sorts of work, and the labourer has to live within the terms of labour-mobility in capitalist society:

> . . . labour is of course in each single case a specific labour, but capital can come into relation with every *determinate* labour; it confronts the *totality* of all labour potentially [*dunamei*], and the particular one it confronts at a given time is accidental. On the other side, the labourer himself is absolutely indifferent to the determinateness of his labour; it has no interest for him as such, but only in as much as it is in fact *labour* and, as such, a use-value for capital (N 296–7; M 217; quotation partially altered).

The capitalist and the labourer are related, not merely in a particular determinateness, but in general. As a member of the class of labourers, the labourer must have abilities to accomplish the different sorts of work which happen to be offered to individuals. Through the adaptation to different kinds of work, the potential develops for labourers to be able to do any kind of job. That potential is what Marx calls the 'general substance' within the labourer.

In real life the labourer consumes the concrete determinateness of the labour already objectified in the means of consumption. This happens through individual consumption undertaken in order to generate abstract labour. This abstract labour is then objectified in order to maintain life and thus reproduce labour as general substance. The general substance or matter (*mater*) within the labourer develops the particular forms of labour-power that exist potentially within it.

Marx's terms 'particular substance' and 'general substance' imply a critique of Hegel's idealism and pseudo-historicism as found in his discussion of the 'relation of substantiality' in the *Logic*:

> The necessary is in itself *absolute relation*, i.e. the developed process . . . in which the relation also supersedes itself to absolute identity [= form].
>
> In its immediate form it is the relation of *substantiality* and *accidentality*. The absolute self-identity of this relation is *Substance* as such, which as necessity is the negativity of this form of inwardness, and thus posits itself as *actuality*, but which is the *negativity* of this outward thing. In this negativity, the actuality as immediate is only an *accidental thing* which through this simple possibility transits into actuality; a *transition* which is the substantial identity as *form-activity* (sect. 150).[19]

Hegel insists that 'substance' is determined as 'necessity', 'subject' and 'absolute *form*' (sect. 149), and it becomes 'actuality' through 'concern' or 'thing' (*Sache* = *telos*), 'activity' (*Tätigkeit* = *archē*) and 'condition' (*Bedingung* = *hylē*). Does his analysis apply to the labour-process or to the valorisation-process? In fact he makes no valid distinction but rather confuses the two.

Marx resolves this confusion by distinguishing 'form' and 'substance'. For him 'subject' is not 'substance' but 'form', both in the labour-process and in the valorisation-process, though the term 'form' has different senses in each process, as we have already seen. The 'form' in the labour-process is the producer, and its opposite is 'matter', which signifies the means of production. The other 'form' occurs in the valorisation-process, where it is understood to be capital or the capitalist, its personification, the opposite of which is 'content' or capital. The capitalist ascribes to concrete things the abstraction capital-value when they are in their productive metamorphoses.

However, Hegel mistakes 'relation' and 'process' for 'substance'. Indeed the relation of exchange becomes independent for him as value and then as a 'subject' itself, conceived apart from the persons who generate it. But 'substance' does not become 'subject'; rather it grounds value, and value subsists as 'substance'. The process in which the relation of private exchange becomes alienated as value is simultaneously accompanied by a process of consumption in which concrete labour is transformed into 'labour in general', the social substance of value. Capital-value as a subject in the economic process alters the particular natural substances in which it appears in order to maintain its subjective identity as value grounded on the social substance, labour in general, which is materialised by the labourer in natural substances.

Hegel's identification of 'substance' with 'subject' is derived from his idealism. He evidently thinks that the whole world or cosmos is the creation of 'substance' through its activity in knowing itself. Substance is 'knowing' (*Wissen*), and therefore it is ideal *par excellence*. It proves itself through its special activity, 'knowing'. Substance as 'knowing' becomes 'subject' through knowing itself. Therefore, according to Hegel, everything in the cosmos is essentially the existence of the ideal.

The development or 'becoming' of 'substance' into 'subject' as outlined by Hegel corresponds to the bourgeois economic system, in which the value-consciousness of real people rules as an idea over natural substances. To this consciousness, everything appears to be determined by value. The transformation of the product into the commodity appears in an inverted way as if value as 'substance' in the product were a 'subject', whereas value is actually the alienation of the exchange-relation between the products of concrete labour, and social substance is concrete labour made abstract as labour in general. That is the real reason why Hegel says that 'substance' is 'subject'.

In the section from the *Logic* cited above, Hegel grasps that 'relation' becomes 'process', 'substance' and 'actuality'. Together they are 'subject'. Indeed, he does not make a clear distinction between 'substance' and 'subject', but presumes that 'substance' becomes 'subject' through positing itself.

By contrast, Marx distinguishes 'substance' from 'subject'. 'Subject' for him is the relation of value or 'form', which is based on abstract labour as social substance. Once money has been generated historically, the relation of value is formed between commodities and money, and it vanishes after exchange. Value requires the social substance from which it is derived. In changing shape within the relation of value, capital also changes its natural substance or use-value in which social substance is embodied. The capitalist as the personification of capital carries out a role of identifying capital as value in relation to its various shapes. With respect to the distinction between 'substance' and 'subject', Marx writes:

> For their part, the raw materials and the instrument are preserved not in their form [*Form*] but in their [natural] substance [*Substanz*], through the simple relation that the instrument as instrument is used and raw material is posited as raw material of labour, through the simple process that they come in contact with labour, being posited as its means and object and thus an objectification of living labour, moments of labour itself; and considered economically, their [social] substance is objectified labour-time (N 360, M 271; quotation partially altered).

Living labour preserves natural substance in the labour-process. It works as 'subject', carrying out material changes, for instance, from cotton to yarn, then to textiles and eventually to clothing. The '*external form* of its natural substance' (N 360, M 271), i.e. raw materials, is consumed and abstracted as 'accidental' (*zufällig*) (N 360, M 272) by living labour, and so it comes to represent an increase in wealth.

However in the valorisation-process, where labour is subsumed under capital as general substance, living labour has the twofold character of objectifying new value (V + S) and preserving old value in constant capital (C). The capitalist, or capital consciousness, commands the labourer to objectify more value than has been objectified in the labourer's own labour-power, and at the same time, to maintain the labour already objectified in the means of production without further reward.

The capital-form, however, is historical, and the capitalist is historically a particular type of individual. Capital is inevitably innovative in technology, because of the drive to obtain increasing profits, and it tends to remove living labour from the process of production. Unawares it makes a transcendence of itself possible as it approaches an extreme point at which no living labour exists in the process of production. Capital is a historical form grounded essentially on social substance. Notwithstanding this, it also repels the very source of social substance, living labour, by expelling it from the economic process. Capital tends to undermine its own 'ground' through its dynamic development.

Component parts of capital and 'the whole and the parts'

Marx now advances from the labour-process to the valorisation-process. He writes:

> Hitherto, capital has been regarded from its material side as a *simple production process*. But, from the side of its formal determinateness, this process is the *self-valorization process* [*Selbstverwertungsprozess*]. Self-valorization includes preservation of the prior value, as well as its multiplication (N 310–11, M 229; quotation partially altered).

This order of analysis, from material relation to formal determinateness, appears in Hegel's *Logic*:

> The Essence must *appear*. Its semblance in it is the transcendence of it to immediacy. While as reflection-on-itself the immediacy is *subsistence* (matter) [*Bestehen* (*Materie*)], it is also *form*, reflection-on-other, subsistence which *transcends itself* (sect. 131; quotation partially altered).

Marx then considers the forms of existence in which capital appears and the contents or use-values to which these forms of capital or value relate. Capital first appears in the form of money, then transforms itself into a 'material mode of existence' (N 313, M 231; quotation partially altered), i.e. the elements of production, and it changes its shape in the product. Therefore: 'The different modes of existence of values were pure semblance [*Schein*]; value itself formed constantly self-identical essence within their disappearance' (N 312, M 231).

Money-capital is transformed into production-capital, and the whole of money-capital is now dissolved into several parts. However, the various modes of existence are semblance (*Schein*). They are in fact forms of appearance of capital-value, because capital maintains its character as value through a metamorphosis of the elements of production into products and then to commodities and money.

The determinations 'semblance' and 'appearance' mentioned by Hegel are also relevant to Marx's discussion:

> Existence, posited in its contradiction, is Appearance [*Erscheinung*]. Appearance is not to be confused with a mere Semblance. Semblance is the proximate truth of Being or Immediacy. The immediate is not what, as we suppose, is something independent, resting on itself, but a mere Semblance, and as such it is summarized in the simplicity of the essence which is in itself (sect. 131, Z; quotation largely altered).[20]

The immediacy and independence of existence are mere 'semblance'. When semblance is mediated with 'essence', it becomes 'appearance'. Marx adopts this logic when he writes that various material modes of existence are 'semblance'. If these material things become products, they persist within their identity as value. They appear as various parts of the whole of capital-value: 'The only process in relation to value [is] that it once appears as a whole [*ein Ganzes*], unity; then as division of this unity into determinate amount [*Anzahl*]; finally, as sum [*Summe*]' (N 314, M 232).

In that way money as capital appears at first as qualitatively the same, a whole or unity. Then it is differentiated into various forms, namely materials for labour, instruments of labour and human labour-power. Finally the 'component parts' (*Bestandteile*) (N 314, M 232; quotation largely altered), of capital are united again into one sum through productive consumption. The way in which Marx traces the transformation of capital-value comes from Hegel's discussion of 'the whole and the parts' in his *Logic*:

> The *immediate* relation is that of the Whole [*das Ganzes*] and *the Parts* [*die Teile*]. The content [*Inhalt*] is the whole, and *consists* of the parts (the form) [*Form*], its counterpart. The parts are diverse one from another and independent. But they are parts, only in their identical relation to one another, or in so far as, being taken together, they constitute the whole (sect. 135; quotation partially altered).[21]

At first glance Marx's usage is the same as Hegel's. However, if we examine it carefully, we see that the two are different at a crucial point. Hegel defines 'content' as equivalent to the whole, and 'form' as equivalent to the parts. By contrast, Marx links 'content' to the parts, and 'form' to the whole. As already indicated, Hegel speculates that 'substance', 'matter' and 'content' are subsumed under 'form', one by one. This constitutes a complex structure in which 'form' is the dominant 'subject', without noting the different kinds of form. Hegel fails to analyse the three kinds of 'form' that appear in 'form and substance', 'form and content', and 'form and matter'. As trans-historical categories, the final pair constitutes 'content'. Hegel's account is misleading, because 'form' is changed from the trans-historical to the historical. 'Content' is then mistaken for something historical.

In economic terms, Hegel indicates that 'content' changes from use-value to value and that 'form' becomes the mode of existence of value. By contrast, Marx claims that 'content' is use-value or, strictly defined, use-value in the commodity, and that 'form' is value, strictly defined, value in money. Therefore form or the abstract whole of capital-value appears in different factors of production. As we will see later, Marx is able to grasp the law of appropriation by making use of the terms 'form' and 'content', each of which changes into the other. Hegel's failure to distinguish between the two sorts of 'form' — historical and trans-historical — results in his pseudo-naturalism[22] and pseudo-historicism.

Manifestation as the force of capital and 'force and its manifestation'

In the 'Chapter on Capital' Marx traces the process of development of capital from its origin in money, through successive transformations as factors of production, then products and so to money ($M-C(L_a+P_m)$ . . . P . . . $C'-M'$), i.e. the circuit of money-capital or circulating capital (N 250–66, M 173–88). He then analyses the exchange between capital and labour (N 266–97, M 188–217), considers the labour-process (N 297–310, M 218–29), grasps the valorisation process (N 310–26, M 229–42) and takes up the first theories of surplus-value (*Ur-Theorien*) (N 326–33, M 242–8). After that, he defines the concept of relative surplus-value (N 333–53, M 248–66). In the two-part 'Results of the Immediate Process of Production' (N 366–401, M 277–309; N 423–34, M 336–45) he studies the motives for, and results of, capitalist investment in machinery.[23]

The following passage concerning the twofold character of

labour deserves examination because of its relationship to Hegel's *Logic*:

> Like every other natural or social force of labour, unless it is the product of previous labour, or of such previous labour as does not need to be repeated (e.g. the historical development of the worker etc.), this animating natural force of labour [*Naturkraft der Arbeit*] — namely, that by using the material and instrument, it preserves them in one or other form, including the labour objectified in them, their exchange-value — becomes a *force of capital* [*Kraft des Kapitals*], not of labour. Hence not paid for by capital. As little as the labourer is paid for the fact that he can think etc. . . . (N 358, M 270; quotation partially altered).

As it is under the command of the capitalist that living labour consumes productively the means of production and thus produces 'a substance with another form' (N 312, M 230), as well as reproducing the labour already objectified in itself, so the natural force in labour manifests itself as if it were a part of capital, a force in capital: 'This preserving force of labour therefore appears as the *self-preserving force* of capital [*Selbsterhaltungskraft*]' (N 364, M 275). 'Force and its manifestation' evidently suggests to Marx a way of seeing through this inversion, when the force in labour appears as a force in capital:

> The Manifestation of Force [*Ihre Äusserung*] itself is the transcendence of variety of the two sides, which is present in this relation, and is positing of identity, which *in itself* constitutes the content. The truth of Force and Manifestation therefore is the relation, in which the two sides are distinguished only as *inward* and *outward* (sect. 137; quotation largely altered).
>
> Through the manifestation of force, the inward is *posited* in existence; this *positing* is the *mediation* through empty abstractions; the inward disappears in itself to *immediacy* . . . (sect. 141; quotation largely altered).[24]

Hegel's logic in the second of these two quotations is applied by Marx to explain how the force in labour, the 'inward', is posited in the 'outward' existence of the product. This positing of the product, however, is mediated or structured by capital, and the force in labour disappears as such, but is manifested as the force in capital.

On the first level at which the labour-process is considered by Marx, 'content' is outwardly opposed to 'form', but on the level of the twofold character of labour, the two are mediated inwardly. This happens in the human body or *archē*, which is alienated from *telos*. The human body actualises the capitalist *telos* by acting as its agent. In relation to *hylē* as such, it produces material wealth or 'content'. As agent for the value-consciousness of the capitalist, it objectifies new value (V + S) and preserves the old constant capital or 'form' (C). In carrying out a metabolism with nature, this twofold *archē* of wage-labour is a factor in capital mediating its relations. Therefore the force which labour actualises with respect to nature is inverted when it appears as the force of capital.

Surplus capital and 'actuality'

After the first part of his 'Results of the Process of Production', in its first variant, Marx outlines the following plan:

The Process of Realisation of Capital — One
Results of the Process of Production — Two
The Process of Realisation of Capital — Two
The Formation of the General Rate of Profit
The Process of Reproduction through Exchanges
The Process of Realisation of Capital — Three
Surplus Product and Surplus Capital
The Conversion of the Law of Appropriation
The Reproduction of the Capital Relation
Pre-capitalist Economic Formations (See pp. 143–4 below, items 9–180)

Here Marx's use of Hegel's *Logic* is focused on the accumulation of capital through primitive accumulation. The accumulation of capital consists of:

1. surplus product and surplus capital (N 450–6, M 360–5);
2. the conversion of the law of appropriation (N 456–8, M 365–7);
3. the reproduction of the capital relation (N 458, M 367).

In Part One of the 'Results' Marx brings the surplus product into focus as a result of the immediate process of production under capital. Surplus products, which are in fact the result of labour viewed from the standpoint of the wage-labourer, are but a stage in the transformation of capital into surplus-capital and are funds for the reproduction of the capital–labour relationship.

In the *Grundrisse* Marx uses Hegel's *Logic* when he writes about alienated labour producing a surplus product. In doing this he refers to a previous discussion in his *Economic and philosophical manuscripts (1844)*:

> When labour is considered from the standpoint of labour itself [*Vom Standpunkt der Arbeit aus betrachtet*], it therefore now appears as acting [*tätig*] in the process of production in such a way that it simultaneously repulses its actualization [*Verwirklichung*] in objective conditions as alien [*fremd*] reality, and hence posits itself as insubstantial, as mere penurious labour-power [*Arbeitsvermögen*] in the face of this reality which is alienated [*entfremdet*] from it, belonging not to it, but to others; that it posits its own actuality not as being-for-itself [*Sein für sich*], but as simple being for other [*blosses Sein für andres*], and hence also as simple other-being [*Anderssein*] or being of others opposite to itself. This actualization process [*Verwirklichungsprocess*] of labour is at the same time the de-actualization process [*Entwirklichungsprocess*] of labour . . . It returns back into itself as the simple possibility [*blosse Möglichkeit*] of value-positing [*Wertsetzung*] or valorization (N 454, M 363; quotation largely altered).

In the *Economic and philosophical manuscripts (1844)* Marx uses a descending analytical method to explicate the concept alienated labour, in order to inquire into its real cause and result — actual alienated labour, modern private property and capital. He analyses the alienated relation of separation between the product of labour and labour itself at the end of the process of production. Though capital appears as the cause of alienated labour or modern private property, he concludes that alienated labour is the real cause of modern private property or capital. In other words, the labourer, the propertyless worker, is the cause, and the non-labourer or property-owner is its effect. Once this relationship between the labourer and the non-labourer is established historically, the relationship appears theoretically in inverted form — capital as cause and alienated labour as effect. At the close of the first of his 1844 manuscripts, Marx writes that he will consider the relation of the non-labourer or capitalist to the labourer from the standpoint of the capitalist. He fulfils this when he considers the conversion of the law of appropriation.

The quotation from the *Grundrisse* cited above demonstrates that Marx's basic view of alienated labour as the cause of capital had not changed since 1844. An extract from the *Economic and philosophical manuscripts (1844)* cited below shows a continuity between those manuscripts and the *Grundrisse* that includes basic terminology:

> The product of labour is labour embodied and made material [*sachlich gemacht hat*] in an object, it is the *objectification* [*Vergegenständlichung*] of labour. The actualization [*Verwirklichung*] of labour is its objectification. In the sphere of national economy this actualization of labour appears as a *loss of actuality* [*Entwirklichung*] for the labourer, objectification as *loss of and bondage to the object*, and appropriation as *alienation* [*Entfremdung*], as *exteriorization* [*Entäusserung*].[25]

Using this understanding of alienated labour, Marx mounts a critique of Hegel in his third manuscript of 1844 as follows:

> . . . in grasping the *positive* significance of the negation which has relation to itself, even if once again in alienated form, Hegel grasps man's self-alienation, exteriorization of being, loss of objectivity and loss of actuality [*Entwirklichung*] as self-appropriation [*Selbstgewinnung*], expression of being, objectification and actualization [*Verwirklichung*]. In short, he sees labour — within abstraction — as man's *act of self-creation* and man's relation to himself as an alien being and the manifestation of himself as an alien being as the emergence of *species-consciousness* and *species-life*.[26]

Therefore labour in the bourgeois economic system is alienated labour. Marx's conception of labour demonstrates not only a critique of Adam Smith's view of labour — that it is by nature disutility or sacrifice which 'man' must make in order to obtain the utility of the product — but also a critique of Hegel, who appropriates Smith's view of labour without critical assessment: 'Hegel adopts the standpoint of modern national economy.'[27]

Like Smith, Hegel cannot have had any insight into the historical form of labour that Marx identifies as alienated labour. The loss of actuality of labour appears to Hegel as the actualisation of labour. Marx's critique of Hegel's view of labour in the *Economic and philosophical manuscripts (1844)* relates Hegel's work in the *Phenomenology of spirit* to Smith's theory of the division of labour. Hegel writes:

> But, in the general substance [*die allgemeine Substanz*], the individual has this *form* of subsistence not only for his activity as such, but no less also for the *content* of that activity; what he does *is* the skill and customary practice of all. This content, in so far as it is completely particularized, is, in its actual existence, confined within the framework of the activity of all. The *labour* [*Arbeit*] of the individual for his own needs is just as much a satisfaction of the needs of others as of his own, and the satisfaction of his own needs he obtains only through the labour of others. As the individual [*das Einzelne*] in his *individual* labour [*seine einzelne Arbeit*] already *unconsciously* [*bewusstlos*] performs a *general* labour [*ein allgemeine Arbeit*], so again he also performs the general labour as his *conscious* [*bewusst*] object.[28]

Smith's view of the division of labour and private exchange in an economic system, in which individuals work one-sidedly and consume multifariously, has been appropriated by Hegel in his *Phenomenology*: firstly, individual labourers are unconscious of the fact that their divided labours are articulated through private exchange into social labour or 'general labour', on which all the members of society are dependent; secondly, the 'general labour' of which they are aware is labour that produces use-value for others and therefore exchange-value; in short, labour which produces commodities.

Hegel's notion of labour implies that it is abstracted or alienated labour. This abstraction or alienation arises from the relationship of private exchange which divides and then links production and consumption. Human labour is further abstracted into 'labour in general' and separated into physical and mental aspects. For Hegel the dominant form of labour is abstract or mental labour which subsumes concrete or physical labour under itself. Concrete labour can exist or be significant only within the sphere of mental labour. Hegel's 'idea' is in fact abstract or mental labour, i.e. value-consciousness. In Smith's *The wealth of nations*, Hegel sees nothing but the world of commodities.

By contrast, in the labour which produces commodities Marx

sees a loss of actuality, whereas Hegel finds the actuality of labour there. In the *Phenomenology* Marx sees a philosophisation of Smith's economic vision of commercial society or civilised society, which, so Smith predicts, never fails to emerge from feudal or mercantile systems. Hence Marx concludes in the *Economic and philosophical manuscripts (1844)* that 'Hegel adopts the standpoint of modern national economy'. In that way Marx's vision of the loss of actuality of the labourer is based on his critique of Smith and Hegel in the manuscripts of 1844.

Moreover in his manuscripts of 1844 Marx criticises and rearranges Hegel's definition of 'actuality' (*Wirklichkeit*). We see this in his consideration of the labour-process and the valorisation process. Hegel translates Aristotle's theory of causation into a theory of actuality: *hylē* is changed to 'condition' (*Bedingung*), *archē* to 'activity' (*Tätigkeit*), *telos* to 'concern' or 'thing' (*Sache*). In the paragraph cited above, the key words 'activity' and 'condition' are used. Marx associates commodity-production and the loss of actuality with Hegel's exposition of 'actuality' in the Doctrine of Essence. The term 'thing' (*Sache*) is significant in this passage from the *Grundrisse*:

> Labour-power has appropriated for itself only the subjective conditions [*Bedingungen*] of necessary labour — the means of subsistence for actively producing labour-power, i.e. for its reproduction as mere labour-power separated from the conditions of its actualization [*Verwirklichung*] — and it has posited these conditions themselves as *things* [*Sachen*], *values* [*Werte*], which confront in it an alien, commanding personification (N 452–3, M 362; quotation partially altered).

The wage-labourer produces under the command of the capitalist. This even includes the production of the 'necessary product', the reproduction fund for the wage-labourer, the fund for the reproduction of labour-power. This is the property of the capitalist as 'thing' or value, i.e. the variable capital with which the capitalist rules the wage-labourer in the process of production. In that context Hegel's term 'thing' (*Sache*) is diverted by Marx into another sense. Hegel has taken over Aristotle's *telos* and redefined it as *Sache*, first of all in the subjective sense of 'concern'. When this 'concern' is actualised through 'activity' and 'condition', it becomes an objective 'thing'. In Hegel's *Sache* Marx sees the capitalist's purpose and will, i.e. the value-consciousness that aims for an increase in capital-value, i.e. the profit motive. Marx calls the actualisation of the profit motive *Sache*, and he defines the circumstances where *Sache* is transformed into 'conditions' as 'objective conditions' (*sachliche Bedingungen*) (N 453, M 362; N 454, M 364). For Marx reification (*Versachlichung*) (N 160, M 93) refers to the situation in which value-consciousness, including capitalist consciousness, is reified in matter or a material substance, the commodity.[29]

As we have seen before, Marx penetrates Hegel's confusion concerning the trans-historical and the historical, typically shown in Marx's demonstration of 'substance' as 'subject' (*natura naturans*) or 'form'. In contrast to Hegel, Marx defines 'form' as historical *par excellence*, so it is *de facto* reified value which appears as 'eternal subject'. One of the main themes of his critique of political economy is the genesis of the two 'forms', value and capital.

Hegel defines the three terms 'condition', 'concern' (*Sache*) and 'activity' as follows: 'Whatever is necessary is through an *Other*, which is broken up into the *mediating ground* (the Concern [*Sache*] and the Activity) and an *immediate* actuality or an accidental circumstance, which is at the same time condition' (sect. 149).[30] For Hegel 'condition' is immediate actuality, and 'condition' (*hylē*) is mediated through two subjective things, 'concern' (*telos*) and 'activity' (*archē*), as it is actualised as a product. In this view, 'concern' and 'activity' are immediately related, so their subjective factors are not alienated, as they are in alienated labour. Marx takes over Hegel's view in his analysis of the labour-process in general.

However, Marx considers another process of valorisation, in which 'concern' and 'activity' are separated between capitalists and wage-labourers, with 'conditions' belonging to capitalists. Then 'concern' changes into a consciousness that is devoted to producing a surplus and increasing the value of capital, and at the same time it incarnates itself in 'conditions'. In the relation between the surplus product and the wage-labourer, who is alienated from the surplus product because it is a mere effect or result of capitalist production, reification (*Versachlichung*) recurs. By 'objective conditions' Marx means that in the valorisation process 'concern' (*Sache*) becomes the mental labour of the capitalist concerned with increasing the value of capital, and 'activity' is the labourer's physical labour. 'Conditions' become the 'thing' (*Sache*) in which the 'concern' of the capitalist is materialised. Therefore 'thing' and 'conditions', both of which belong to the capitalist, are linked and appear as 'immediate actuality', and 'activity' appears as 'simple possibility' (N 454, M 363).

The conversion of the law of appropriation and 'absolute necessity'

Marx then considers the surplus product 'from the standpoint of capital' (N 456, M 365). He demonstrates the first conversion of the law of appropriation. At the beginning of the 'Chapter on Capital' in the *Grundrisse*, money, which is capital in potentiality, is presupposed in such a way that it is accumulated labour belonging only to the owner of labour-power. Money or 'the original non-surplus capital' (*das ursprüngliche — Nicht-Surpluscapital — sic*) (N 455, M 365; quotation partially altered) produces '*surplus capital I*' (N 456, M 365) at the end of the first circuit (*Kreislauf*), in which a commodity is exchanged for money and that money for another commodity. At the beginning of the second circuit, in which money is exchanged for a commodity and that commodity for more money, 'surplus capital I' (S) is divided into $S_c + S_v$ in proportion to the original capital. The exchange between surplus variable capital (S_v) and labour-power, from the standpoint of the labouring class as a whole, is not an exchange of anything other than their own labour. What the capitalist gives to the labourer is merely a return of the labourer's own surplus labour. The capitalist purchases new labour-power with surplus variable capital (S_v) or old surplus labour. This purchase converts the law of appropriation based on the labourer's own labour into a 'formal' exchange (N 456, M 365).

Secondly, Marx shows how the law of appropriation based on the 'exchange of equivalents' (N 457, M 366) is transformed into its opposite. At the end of the second circuit, 'surplus capital I' appropriates the product, which is analysed as $S_c + S_v + S_s$. 'Surplus capital I' has then purchased S_s, i.e. 'surplus capital II' (N 457, M 366). At the starting point of the circuit, money is presumed to become capital through the exchange of equivalents. However, 'surplus capital II' is merely that which 'surplus capital I' has posited. In other words, 'surplus capital II' is obtained from its non-equivalent, 'surplus value I'. Thus the law of appropriation based on the exchange of equivalents has become 'mere semblance' (*blosser Schein*) (N 458, M 367) and has been converted into its opposite:

> The right of property converts [*umschlagen*], on one side, into the right to appropriate alien labour, and on the other, the duty of respecting the product of one's own labour, and one's own labour itself, as values belonging to others. The exchange of equivalents, however, which appears as the original operation, an operation to which the right of property gave legal expression, has turned round in such a way as it is exchanged only into semblance [*nur zum Schein ausgetauscht wird*] (N 458, M 367; quotation largely altered).

The exchange between capital and labour appears at first as a simple exchange between equivalents created by the labourer's own labour. The purpose of the exchange, from the standpoint of the wage-labourer, is to obtain use-value for individual consumption. However, from the standpoint of the capitalist, the purpose of the exchange does not appear as simple use-value, but as a specific use-value which realises 'form as content' or 'form' as value, which becomes the 'content' of the exchange. The special use-value of labour-power is the specific use-value realised in valorisation. The capitalist aims to appropriate labour on the basis of the law of the exchange of equivalents. Strictly defined, alien labour includes an increase over necessary labour, so it is alien surplus-labour, owned by the capitalist.

In the capitalist's appropriation of alien surplus-labour, labour-power is 'simple possibility' (N 454, M 363). It is able to objectify surplus-labour only through its connection with the capitalist means of production ('immediate actuality') or the 'conditions' in which the capitalist's 'concern' (*Sache*) or profit motive is embodied. Moreover labour-power is alienated from the means of consumption (another 'immediate actuality') which also belongs to the capitalist. In the process of capitalist production, 'simple possibility' as labour-power, combined with 'actuality' as means of production, becomes superseded by one of the elements of 'actuality' as the product. In the process of individual consumption, 'mere possibility' as labour-power is reproduced as general substance through the consumption of another 'actuality' as means of subsistence. This is subsumed under capitalist production. The presuppositions 'possibility' and 'actuality', which have been in an 'external' relationship, are now posited as the 'internal' results of the process of production.

This method of grasping capitalist production is derived from Hegel's 'absolute necessity' as follows:

> Thus *form* [*Form*] in its realization has penetrated all its differences and made itself transparent and is, as *absolute necessity* [*absolute Notwendigkeit*], only this simple *self-identity of being in its negation*, or in *essence*. — The difference of *content* [*Inhalt*] and form itself has also vanished; for that unity of possibility in actuality [*Einheit der Möglichkeit in der Wirklichkeit*], and conversely, is the *form* which in its determinateness or in positedness is indifferent [*gleichgültig*] towards itself, is the *thing filled with content* [*inhaltsvolle Sache*], in which the form of necessity ran its external course . . . But the dissolution of this difference is absolute necessity whose content is this difference which in this necessity penetrates itself . . . Absolute necessity is thus the *reflection or form of the absolute*: the unity of being and essence, simple immediacy that is absolute negativity. Consequently, *on the one hand*, its differences do not exist as determinations of reflection, but *as existing multiplicity* or differentiated actuality which has the shape of others independent against one another. *On the other hand*, since its relation is absolute identity, it is the *absolute conversion* [*das absolute Umkehren*] of its actuality into its possibility and of its possibility into actuality.[31]

In the above quotation Hegel asserts that the form of absolute necessity, which penetrates (*durchdringen*) all content, is 'thing filled with content'. 'Thing' (*Sache*) on this level is capitalist concern or value-consciousness which aims to valorise itself through its own metamorphoses. As previously demonstrated in this chapter, the content or use-value of capital is transformed (*umschlagen*) into its 'form' or value in three phases — the valorisation process, the production of relative surplus-value and the twofold character of labour. These are results which capital realises at the end of the process of production. All of the 'contents' as use-values are now mediated and thus full of 'the concern [*Sache*] of capital' (N 356, M 268; quotation partially altered). The 'contents' are penetrated by the 'form', which has become 'form as content'.

This 'absolute conversion' (*absolute Umkehren*) between 'possibility' and 'actuality' in the 'Major Logic' corresponds to 'absolute conversion' (*das absolute Umschlagen*) (sect. 151) in the 'Minor Logic'. Therefore *Umkehren* is equivalent to *Umschlagen*, the term used by Marx in his exposition of the way in which the law of appropriation is converted.

This twofold conversion of the law of appropriation — capitalist's money = labourer's surplus-labour, and exchange of equivalents = exchange of non-equivalents — is also related to Hegel's definitions of 'form' and 'content'. As noted above, the capitalist realises a purpose, the appropriation of alien surplus-labour, through the conversion of the 'content' of capital into 'form' in three phases — the valorisation process, the production of relative surplus-value and the twofold character of labour (creator of new values and preserver of old). As a result, surplus-value becomes surplus-capital at the beginning of the second circuit: $M_1 - C - C - M_2$, $M_2 > M_1$.

Now Marx brings the exchange between surplus variable capital (a part of surplus capital) and labour-power into focus. Surplus variable capital is the 'form' into which the 'content' or use-value of labour-power has been converted. The 'form' now rules as the power of capitalists over 'content', labour-power as use-value. In capitalist production, 'form' is converted into 'content' and vice versa. This logic corresponds to the conversion of the law of appropriation. The exchange of capital with labour-power, presupposed as a simple form of exchange, is in fact a specific kind of exchange in which the 'content' is the 'form', i.e. value. 'Form as content' is realised through the appropriation of alien surplus-labour, i.e. the labourer's own surplus.

Surplus-labour becomes surplus-capital through the action of the capitalist, who is a seller ($C' - M'$). This act in the sphere of circulation converts 'content' as commodity into 'form' as money. Therefore the law of appropriation based on the labourer's own labour is converted into its opposite, an exchange of alien labour in the 'form' of surplus variable capital with alien labour as use-value, the content of labour-power. Here again we see the conversion of 'form' into 'content'.

The exchange of capital with labour-power results in the second conversion of the law of appropriation. This happens at the end of the second circuit (*Kreislauf*) of money-capital, where capital has absorbed alien surplus-value. At the beginning of the first circuit of money-capital, money, in order to become capital, is presupposed as the accumulated labour of its owner. Therefore it might be possible for the owner of the labour to allege that surplus-value at the end of the first circuit of money-capital is the result of the labourer's own activity.

But what is the case with respect to surplus-value at the end of the second circuit of money-capital? It is not the result of the labourer's own activity, but is rather alien surplus-labour, which has become the property of the capitalist. The capitalist has obtained it using labour appropriated at the end of the first circuit. Alien surplus-labour becomes surplus capital, which then produces alien surplus-labour. Capital is an accumulation of alien surplus-labour.

The law of appropriation based on the exchange of equivalents is thus converted into its opposite. The conversion is absolute and necessary, because the external unity of 'form' and 'content' in simple exchange has been transformed into 'form as content' or capital. In capital's exchange with labour-power, 'form' has become determinate 'content', 'content' is penetrated throughout by 'form'. Therefore the 'form' of simple exchange based on the labourer's own labour has become 'form without content', and the exchange of equivalents has also changed into a 'mere semblance' (*blosse Schein*) (N 458, M 367).

In his demonstration of the conversion of the law of appropriation in *Capital*, Marx takes over Hegel's 'absolute necessity':

> The relation of exchange between capitalist and labourer becomes a simple semblance [*blosse Schein*] belonging only to the process of circulation, it becomes a mere form [*Form*], which is alien to the content [*Inhalt*] of the transaction itself, and merely mystifies it. The constant sale and purchase of labour-power is the form [*Form*]; the content [*Inhalt*] is the constant appropriation by the capitalist, without equivalent, of a portion of the labour of others which has already been objectified, and his repeated exchange of this labour for the greater quantity of the living labour of others.[32]

The reproduction of the capital relation and 'causality'

After linking the twofold conversion of the law of appropriation to the 'absolute conversion' between 'form' and 'content' under 'absolute necessity', Marx advances to the reproduction of the capital-relation, referring to 'causality' at the end of Hegel's Doctrine of Essence.

Marx writes about the results of the process of production of capital from the standpoint of reproduction: 'Each reproduces itself, by reproducing its other [*sein Andres*], its negation. The capitalist produces labour as alien; labour produces the product as alien. The capitalist produces the labourer, and the labourer the capitalist etc.' (N 458, M 367). Because of the labourer's alienation from the product of labour (*hylē* as such), the labourer has to externalise (*entäussern*) labour-power as mere 'possibility' (*archē*), and the labourer works as alien labour. Consequently the product of the labourer belongs to another, the capitalist, and the labourer must put labour-power up for sale again. The capitalist as non-labourer, the personification of the 'concern of capital' or the alienated social *eidos*, rules over the labour of others. The capitalist appropriates the product, in which surplus-labour is embodied, and makes it a fund for commanding the labour of others once again. Each capitalist and labourer is a 'being-for-itself' (*Fürsichsein*): '. . . capital in its Being-for-itself is the *capitalist* . . . As a labourer he is nothing more than labour in its Being-for-itself' (N 303–4, M 223).

Both the capitalist and the labourer exist only in relation to each other. Marx characterises the capitalist as 'selfish value' (*selbstischer Wert*) (N 303, M 223; quotation partially altered), referring to the *Economic and philosophical manuscripts (1844)*, in which he points out that what Hegel defines as 'self' in the *Phenomenology* is but the 'abstract egoist' or bourgeois.[33] 'Selfish value' is another expression of capitalist value-consciousness which identifies the labourer with variable capital.

But the labourer as an agent for the capitalist not only produces the product of labour, but together with the capitalist reproduces the capital-relation, in which the labourer works as a non-appropriator, and the capitalist as a non-worker and appropriator. The labourer produces poverty for labourers, wealth for capitalists.

In economic relations, according to Marx, results or effects turn into presuppositions or causes. His model of an organic system of circular self-reproduction depends on Hegel's account of 'causality':

> . . . the passive substance itself is *twofold*, namely, an independent *other* [*Anderes*] and also something *presupposed* and in itself already *identical* with the active cause, the action of substance, too, is twofold; it is two actions in one: the transcendence of its *determinedness*, namely, of its condition, or the transcendence of the self-subsistence of the passive substance; and by thus transcending of its identity with the passive substance, it *presupposes* itself or posits itself as *other* [*Anderes*].[34]

Because of the labourer's alienation from wealth as the product of labour, the labourer is formally independent as a commodity-owner. The labourer is a 'simple possibility' or 'passive substance' with respect to wealth. The labourer is also 'other' (*Anderes*), separated from the actual conditions of wealth, and so separated from 'actuality' in the form of the means for production and consumption. In reality the labourer is dependent on another person for the conditions of self-actualisation, so the independence of the labourer is merely a semblance. Labour-power becomes 'active cause' when it is sold to another, and it has a dual effect — producing poverty for itself, and wealth for another.

First critique of Hegel's system

Is the causal relation between capital and labour, in which the result or effect becomes a succeeding presupposition or cause, actually a closed system as defined by Hegel? Is it a progress *ad infinitum*? Marx argues that this is not the case.

After considering the reproduction of the capital-relation in the *Grundrisse*, Marx considers the economic forms which precede capitalist production (N 459–515, M 367–417). In that discussion he offers an implicit criticism of Hegel's 'causality' as an eternal circular movement. Because Marx has already grasped the causal relation between capital and labour, through which the actual conditions of capitalist production are repeatedly reproduced, presupposition or cause is ceaselessly posited by him as a result or effect.

Hegel writes:

> In the finite sphere the *difference* of the form-determinations in their relation is suspended [*stehengeblieben wird*]: cause is alternately determined *also* as what is *posited* or as *effect*; this again has *another* cause, and thus there also generates the progress from effects to causes *ad infinitum* (sect 153; quotation largely altered).[35]

What is posited in the logical past as presupposition is reproduced in the logical present as result. Reproduction is the actuality of labour which reproduces the past in the present. In this logical phase, Marx shares Hegel's view of circular causality.

However, Marx also argues that something else is reproduced in the result besides the logical past. This is the historical past. After demonstrating that the logical past or presupposition is repeatedly reproduced in the logical present or result, Marx inquires, in a methodological way, when and where the original presuppositions were posited. He moves beyond the logical past and investigates the historical origin of the first logical presuppositions, how they arose in the historical past.

Causal reproduction not only brings about the logical past, but it also reveals historical origins buried under the surface appearance of the present. Marx locates the primitive community and primitive accumulation in his discussion of pre-capitalist economic formations, which follows his account of the accumulation of capital (surplus product and surplus capital) and the reproduction of the capital relation. He argues that capitalism is not a closed system, but an open one, in the sense that it arose from certain conditions in the pre-capitalist period and did not generate them itself. In this way Marx offers an implicit critique of Hegel's closed system, the system in which Hegel unconsciously traces the logic of value and capital, albeit in reverse order.

Marx's critique is supplemented by an exposition of the concept 'disposable time' (N 397, M 305), in order to demonstrate that capitalism is also an open system with respect to its future. For Marx capitalism is determined theoretically in such a way that it will eventually cease to operate and hence to exist. Using his work on pre-capitalist economic formations and on disposable time, Marx shows that capitalism has a historical existence — a historical origin and a historical limit.

In discussing 'disposable time', Marx takes up a suggestion from a pamphlet entitled 'The Source and Remedy of the National Difficulties, Deduced from Principles of Political Economy in a Letter to Lord John Russell, 1821',[36] which he had read in 1851. From this pamphlet he quotes the thesis, '*Wealth is disposable time* and nothing more' (N 397, M 305). Disposable time is exclusively appropriated by the capitalist in the form of surplus-value. However, capitalism is a paradoxical system. Individual capitalists increase the productivity of labour in order to obtain extra surplus-value. With this motive as an efficient cause, capitalism as a whole drives itself in such a way that the law of value eventually becomes groundless. This happens because almost all of the product is produced with a decreasing amount of labour, the very basis of the law of value. Therefore capitalism will cease to exist. After capitalism, Marx predicts, a high level of productivity will be controlled by freely associated workers.

Marx writes:

> Labour-power relates to its labour as to an alien, and if capital were willing to pay it *without* making it labour it would enter the bargain with pleasure. Thus its own labour is as alien to it — and it really is, as regards its direction etc. — as are material and instrument. Therefore, the product then appears to it as a combination of alien material, alien instrument and alien labour — as *alien property*, and after production, it has become poorer by the life forces expended, but otherwise begins the drudgery anew, existing as simple subjective labour-power separated from the conditions of its life. The recognition of the products as its own, and the judgement that its separation from the conditions of its actualization [*Verwirklichung*] is improper — forcibly imposed — is an enormous consciousness [*ein enormes Bewusstsein*], itself the product of the mode of production resting on capital, and as much the knell to its doom as, with the slave's consciousness of himself that he *cannot be the property of a third*, with his consciousness as person, slavery vegetates to merely artificial existence and has ceased to be able to prevail as the basis of production (N 462–3, M 370–1; quotation largely altered).

The human subjects who transcend the 'form' surplus-value and arrive at 'disposable time' are the immediate producers. They are organised and trained under the command of capitalists. Step by step they become aware that capitalist property is only what they themselves have produced, and so they are its true owners. The development of this consciousness and enlightenment are related to Hegel's conception of 'master and slave' in the *Phenomenology*.[37] Here we can see how Marx's phenomenology of mind or spirit is grounded on the critique of political economy.

As already noted, the wage-labourer is determined as a twofold existence. The wage-labourer is not only '*archē* as *hylē*' in relation to the capitalist, but '*archē* as *eidos*' in relation to the means of production. Within the labourer's consciousness an antagonistic contradiction arises. This is between being an agent for the capitalist and being a productive person, or between being a producer of value and being a producer of use-value. The labourer shares a value-consciousness with the capitalist in exchange-relations. These are based on the premise that what is exchanged is the product of the labourer's own labour, and that exchange is carried out on the basis of equivalents. However under capitalism, immediate producers are alienated from the results of their labours, and gradually they come to believe that something is amiss. In order to clarify their intuitions, Marx has demonstrated the way that capital proceeds from an exchange between capitalist and labourer. If the immediate producers follow this demonstration, they will know what causes capitalist property, and they will grasp the basis of their intuition that something is amiss. This theoretical recognition results in a new consciousness amongst producers, a consciousness of the possibilities for human freedom.

Marx's treatment of this material at the beginning of the 'Chapter on Capital' is related to Hegel's 'positing reflection', in which the conditions for the transition of money to capital are presupposed. On those presuppositions Marx demonstrates the transition, showing the indispensable conditions for the genesis of capital. After that logical development, he then follows the historical process in which the conditions were actually posited. His task is finished when he discusses pre-capitalist economic formations. In other words the transition from money to capital is now mediated by the pre-capitalist economic formations in which Marx traces the origins of free exchange, free labour-power, free funds and the accumulation of money. In that sense he shows that capitalism is a logico-historical system that is open, by contrast with Hegel's logical system that is closed and timeless.

4

The 'Chapter on Capital' and the Doctrine of Essence, Part Two: 'Particularity of Capital'

Particularity of capital and 'judgement'

Marx has outlined the genesis of capital in general terms from the transition of value to money and thence to capital, thus tracing the process in which capital becomes (*werden*) the 'notion' (*Begriff*). His account concentrates on the exchange between capital and labour, the production of surplus-value and the accumulation of capital. But the representative form of modern capital is industrial capital, which arises from further mediations in the processes of production and circulation, i.e. the circulation of capital. His next task is to trace the way in which capital develops mechanised industry, to give an account of the forms it takes and to analyse its movements in the processes of production and circulation. He covers those topics in the second part of the 'Chapter on Capital' in the *Grundrisse*.

That part of the 'Chapter on Capital' can be divided into three sections, dealing with circulating and fixed capital, as follows:

1. general determinations of circulating and fixed capital (N 516–618, M 417–505);[1]
2. particular determinations of circulating and fixed capital (N 618–721, M 505–97);
3. individual determinations of circulating and fixed capital (N 721–43, M 597–616).

Those three sections correspond to the economic content of the three books of the second volume of *Capital* as follows:

1. 'Circuit of Capital' (*Kreislauf des Kapitals*);

2. 'Turnover of Capital';
3. 'Reproduction of Capital'.

However, it must be noted that the reproduction of capital as Marx traces it in the *Grundrisse* is premised on 'one capital' only, whereas in *Theories of surplus-value* written in 1861–3, 'one capital' is transcended and becomes 'the whole social capital' or 'many capitals'.

The three determinations under consideration here are expressions in terms of circulating and fixed capital that reflect the triadic structure 'generality', 'particularity' and 'individuality' which Marx takes from Hegel.

In 'generality of capital' the circuit of money-capital (M...M′) yields the general determination of capital, and Marx writes that 'circulating capital is the first form of capital' (N 253, M 176). A little later he characterises capital as 'generality' in constant metamorphosis, or as 'identity' which mediates itself with particular natural substances (N 262, M 185).

In 'particularity of capital' Marx defines capital as circulating capital, so long as it moves ceaselessly and increases value. However, it does not circulate formlessly, but takes on particular forms such as conditions for production, commodities and money. However, the value of capital is fixed so long as it is in a particular form. In that sense every capital is fixed capital, or the negation of circulating capital. By using the terms circulating and fixed capital in that unusual way Marx mediates the determination of capital as 'generality'. He does this in order to trace capital in its circuit as money-capital, using the terms fixed and circulating capital in their 'essential' meanings, but he intends to redefine capital and its two aspects as productive capital (P...P).

In the determination of capital as 'individuality' Marx follows the process of reproduction through circulation. In that process the value of capital particularises itself as circulating and fixed capital. These two sorts of capital are mutually transformed in the reproduction and replacement of value and in its valorisation or increase. They become a totality or an 'individual' entity whilst maintaining their differences. In this particularisation through mutual transformation, circulating and fixed capital become 'one'. 'One' becomes 'two', then the 'two' are united again into 'one' with manifold determinations.

In considering the 'individuality' of capital, Marx criticises Smith's theories of profit and interest, found in Chapter 4 of

Book II of *The wealth of nations*, where Smith considers profit in connection with reproduction. For Marx, capital particularises itself into manifold forms, uniting itself into 'one' or an 'individual' when surplus-value results, i.e. profit. Every aspect of capital appears as equally productive, so the theory of profit in the *Grundrisse* is founded on a view of the reproduction of capital through its circulation.

Marx's analysis is related to Hegel's *Logic*, because Hegel writes that 'judgement' (*Ur-Teil* = 'original division') is demonstrated in 'particularizing' (*Besonderung*) (sect. 166, Z), and 'judgement' is an externalisation of a negative moment immanent in the 'notion'. At an extreme, 'particularizing' becomes 'one' or an 'individual' through a mutual transformation of opposite moments. 'The circle of its self-excluding particularization' (sect. 177) in the 'judgement' is equivalent to the 'totality of its *particularizations*' (sect. 191, quotation partially altered) in the 'syllogism'. Marx's demonstration of the reproduction of capital through circulation is founded on the internal logic of Hegel's 'judgement' and 'syllogism'.

The general determination and 'the categorical judgement'

At the beginning of the discussion of the 'Generality of Capital', Marx reflects on the difference between the simple circulation of commodities and money, and the circulation of capital. For Marx the circulation of commodities and money is the 'bad infinity', in which the point of departure is not linked with the end-point, so circulation is 'merely formal' (N 536, M 435). But the circulation of capital is the 'true infinity', in which the point of departure and the end-point are mediated by capitalist value-consciousness as 'content' for its 'form' (*die Inhaltsvolle*) (N 517, M 418). This is another usage of 'form' and 'content' as reciprocal concepts:

> Capital is thus posited as processing value, which is capital in every moment. It is thus posited as *circulating capital*; in every moment capital, and circulating from one determination into the next. The point of return is at the same time the point of departure and vice versa — namely the *capitalist*. Every capital is originally circulating capital (N 536, M 435; quotation partially altered).

Capital is identified by Marx as abstract value as long as it is in the process of circulation. In that process it persists as capital through the metamorphoses that occur between its point of departure and its return. For that reason capital requires a human 'bearer' who recognises this identity — the capitalist:

> As the subject overlapping the different phases of this movement, as value sustaining and multiplying itself in it, as the subject of these metamorphoses proceeding in a circular course — as a capital, as an expanding circle — capital is *circulating capital*. Circulating capital is therefore initially not a *particular* form of capital, but is rather *capital* itself [*das Kapital*], in a further developed aspect, as subject of the movement just described, which it, itself, is as its own valorization process. In this respect, therefore, every capital is *circulating capital* (N 620, M 507; quotation partially altered).

As value in a continual process, every capital is circulating capital, but it is also fixed capital, so long as it retains a specific shape:

> But while capital thus, as the whole of circulation, is *circulating capital*, is the transition from one phase into the other, it is at the same time, within each phase, posited in a specific determinateness, restricted to a particular form, which is the negation of itself as the subject of all the various transformations. Non-circulating capital. *Fixed capital*, actually *fixated* capital, fixated in one of the different particular determinatenesses, phases, through which it must move (N 620–1, M 507; quotation partially altered).

In Marx's 'generality' of circulating and fixed capital we can see capital is by nature circulating capital in the sense that it must undergo ceaseless metamorphosis in order to valorise itself. But it is at the same time fixed capital so long as it is fixated in particular forms. These determinations reveal Marx's dependence on the 'categorical judgement', the first judgement of 'necessity' in Hegel's *Logic*:

> The Judgement of Necessity, i.e. of the identity of the content in its difference, contains in the predicate, partly the *substance* or *nature* of the *subject*, the *concrete* general [*das konkrete*

> *Allgemeine*], the *genus* [*die Gattung*]; partly, while this general also contains the determinateness as negative, the *exclusive* essential determinateness — the *species* [*die Art*]; — this is the *categorical* judgement (sect. 177; quotation partially altered).[2]

In the circuit of production and circulation, capital is determined as 'genus', i.e. every capital is circulating capital. Capital is not, however, 'the concrete general', but 'the abstract general' determination. It also contains a negative determinateness, i.e. the negation of circulating capital. This negation is fixed capital, so capital retains both aspects within itself. This 'generality of capital' corresponds to the 'categorical judgement' in Hegel's *Logic*.

In that way Marx begins with circulation (C), presupposing production (P), and he traces a process in which circulation posits production, and then production posits circulation (C–P–C). Then he traces a reverse process in which production is structured by capital circulation, and circulation then posits production (P–C–P), so each phase contains the mediations of capital from the preceding phases:

> The phases through which capital travels, which form one circuit [*Umlauf*] of capital, begin conceptually with the transformation of money into the conditions of production [M–C($L_p + P_m$)] . . . Now, however, that we begin not with capital in the process of becoming [*werdend*], but capital which has become [*geworden*] . . . (N 618–19, M 505–6; quotation partially altered).[3]

Marx grasps the genesis of capital as a concept, firstly, in tracing the circuit of money-capital (M–C . . . P . . . C′–M′), and then secondly in the circuit of productive capital (P . . . C′–M′–C . . . P). In other words, he follows the process in which capital produces surplus-value and accumulates it as surplus-capital. Then he changes his viewpoint in order to examine the way in which capital structures mechanised production in order to valorise itself.

Because the nature of capital is internalised in the circuit of productive capital, and because capital is grasped as a permanent subject in a circular system of presupposing and positing, Marx's work on capital is connected with 'positing reflection' in Hegel's *Logic*.

The particularising determination and 'the hypothetical judgement'

Marx advances to the 'particularity' of capital, in order to examine Ricardo's definitions of circulating and fixed capital:

> *The same* capital appears in the same business in the two different forms, the *particular modes of existence* of *fixed and circulating*, hence exists doubly. To be fixed or circulating appears as a *particular* determinateness of capital apart from that of being capital. It must, however, proceed to this particularization [*Besonderung*] (N 645, M 529; quotation partially altered).

> The *particular nature of use-value*, in which the value exists, or which now appears as capital's body, here appears as itself a *determinant* of the *form* [*Formbestimmend*] and of the action of capital; as giving one capital a particular attribute [*eine besondre Eigenschaft*] as against another; as particularizing it (N 646, M 530; quotation partially altered).

A single capital divides itself into particular sorts of capital, circulating and fixed. In the 'generality of capital', capital has these two aspects. In its aspect of circulating capital, capital's nature is to transform itself as quickly as possible; but at the same time it is also fixed capital, in that it must remain within a particular form for a shorter or longer period. The 'generality of capital' expresses the two aspects which capital displays when it moves as 'one' capital.

However, when capital is invested in actual conditions of production, those periods must be differentiated, because capital as raw material may remain in that form for some shorter time, whereas it may remain much longer in the form of machinery. Both use-value and value in raw materials are removed wholly and at one time from the process of production when they take on the form of the product. But the value of machinery is transferred to the product only bit by bit, and whilst it is still operating, its use-value remains as a whole during the productive process until the machine is completely used up. Provision for workers (*approvisionnement*), the actual form which wages take, also behaves like raw material in the productive process, and it belongs to circulating capital.

When Marx is considering the 'generality of capital', he calls this process in which capital moves as one capital 'the whole production process of capital' (N 620, M 506) or 'the whole process' (N 673, M 555). But now the whole process has been divided into 'large-scale circulation' and 'small-scale circulation', in which capital moves at different speeds according to the different sorts of use-value in which its value is materialised:

> Small-scale circulation [*die kleine Circulation* — *sic*] between capital and labour-power. This accompanies the production process and appears as contract, exchange, form of intercourse; under the presupposition of which the production process engages itself. The part of capital entering into this circulation — the *approvisionnement* — is circulating capital *par excellence*. It is determined not only in respect to its form; in addition to this, its use-value, i.e. its material determination as product consumable and directly entering into individual consumption, itself constitutes a part of the determination of form.
>
> Large-scale circulation [*die grosse Circulation* — *sic*]; the movement of capital outside the production phase, where its time appears in opposition to labour-time, as circulation-time. From this opposition of capital engaged in the production sphere to capital stepping out of it, the distinction between *fluid* and *fixed capital* is produced. Fixed is that which is fixated in the production process and is consumed within it; comes out of large-scale circulation, certainly, but does not return into it, and, in so far as it circulates, circulates only in order to be consumed in, confined to, the consumption process (N 678, M 559; quotation largely altered).

While, up to now, fixed capital and circulating capital appeared simply as different passing determinations of capital, they have now hardened into two particular modes of its existence [*besondre Existenzweisen*], and circulating capital appears beside fixed capital. Now two particular sorts of capital [*2 besondre Arten Capital*] exist. In so far as one capital [*ein Capital*] is considered in a particular branch of production, it appears as divided into these two portions, or splits into these two sorts of capital in a certain proportion.

The difference within the production process, originally between the means of labour and materials for labour, and finally the product of labour, now appears as circulating capital (the last two) and fixed capital. The distinction of capital in terms of its simply material aspect is now taken into its form itself, and appears as differentiating it (N 702–3, M 579; quotation largely altered).

This whole process corresponds to the 'generality of capital', and small-scale and large-scale circulation are the actual processes in which one capital is particularised and differentiated into two kinds of capital. The value of one capital appears in 'the two particular sorts (*Arten*) of capital', i.e. circulating capital and fixed capital. These are positive and negative aspects of the 'generality of capital'. The positive aspect appears as circulating capital when it is raw material and wage-provision; and the negative aspect appears as fixed capital when it is machinery. This way of comprehending concepts is based on the 'hypothetical judgement' in Hegel's *Logic*:

> According to their substantiality, the two terms receive the shape [*Gestalt*] of independent actuality. Their identity is only *inward*; and thus the actuality of the one [= the subject] is at the same time *not its own*, but the being of *the other* [= the predicate]; — this is the Hypothetical Judgement (sect. 177; quotation largely altered).[4]

As with the preceding 'categorical judgement' Hegel here again equates substantiality with an independent subject. Thinking in economic terms, however, Marx does not take 'subject' to be 'substance'. 'Substance' is objectified labour in a certain material product, and objectified labour is then abstracted through the value-relation from the concrete labour embodied in the product. 'Subject', however, is the 'form' of value which exists in the relation of private exchange and appears to move from one exchange-relation to another. In that way positive and negative aspects of capital are externalised into two outward appearances, circulating and fixed capital.

Marx regards circulating and fixed capital as a development from the component parts of capital in the valorisation process. He divides the whole value of capital into constant capital and variable capital, and in doing so, he refers to Hegel's 'the whole and the parts'. He does the same thing in considering circulating and fixed capital.

In the valorisation process, value and use-value are not yet mediated with respect to capital: '. . . this material side — or, its determination as use-value and as real process — did not at all coincide with its determination of form [= constant and variable capital]' (N 691, M 570; quotation partially altered). Now however:

> . . . with the distinction between circulating capital (raw material and product) and *fixed capital* (means of labour), the distinction of the elements as use-value is posited simultaneously as a distinction within capital as capital, in its determination of form (N 692, M 571; quotation partially altered).

In Marx's consideration of the 'turnover of capital' in the *Grundrisse*, differences in use-value appear to determine the flow of the value of productive capital. The whole value of one capital is particularised into two parts, circulating and fixed capital.

Properties of circulating capital and fixed capital, and 'force and its manifestation'

In the valorisation process Marx grasps that the productive forces of labour are manifested as a force of capital. Using Hegel's 'force and its manifestation', he characterises the properties of circulating and fixed capital as follows:

> . . . in *fixed capital*, the social productive force of labour [is] posited as property [*Eigenschaft*] inherent in capital; *including the scientific power as well as the combination of social forces within the production process, and finally, the skill transposed from direct labour into the machine, into the dead productive force. In circulating capital,* by contrast, the exchange of labours, of the different branches of labour, their interlacing and system-forming, the co-existence of productive labours, appears as a *property of capital* (N 715–16, M 592).

The productive forces of social labour, which are realised with the aid of science, are absorbed into machinery and manifested as a property of fixed capital. Individual labours are combined socially through circulating variable capital in the form of wage-provision. Therefore productive forces, which derive from social relations, are manifested as a property of circulating capital. Marx's analysis of these manifestations of the force of capital as a reification (*Versachlichung*) of the productive forces of labour is related to Hegel's 'the thing and its properties' in the Doctrine of Essence:

> A thing [*ein Ding*] has the property of effecting this or that in another thing and of expressing itself in a peculiar manner in its relation to it. It demonstrates this property only under the condition that the other thing has a corresponding constitution, but at the same time the property is ***proper*** [*eigentümlich*] to the first thing and is its self-identical substrate; it is for this reason that this reflected quality is called ***property*** [*Eigenschalt*].[5]

In Hegel's view a property belongs to the thing itself. But in Marx's contrasting view, what seems to be the property of a thing is in fact a reification (*Versachlichung*) of social labour in the form of scientific power or collective force materialised into things such as machinery or wage-provision. In capitalism those forces are actualised through the objects with which the capitalist is characteristically concerned (*Sache*).

Marx's critical application of Hegel's 'the thing and its properties' to the turnover of capital corresponds to his use of 'force and its manifestation' in considering the valorisation process. Hegel presumes that a thing itself is an independent existence expressing its own properties in relation to other things. Marx criticises this view, suggesting that in the modern economic sphere which Hegel unconsciously describes in abstract terms in the *Logic*, he has been influenced by the British political economists, e.g. Smith and Ricardo. In Marx's view, Hegel's properties of things are not properties of the things as such, but properties that forms of capital in production and circulation have mediated so that they appear in material things.

Marx's critique of Hegel is also applicable to the political economists. They are obsessed with the appearance of the turnover of capital, which displays a ceaseless expansion in material production as the circular process from production through circulation and back to production is repeated. In that process the turnover of productive capital from circulation through production and back to circulation becomes immanent within the turnover of productive capital. Consequently the political economists mistake the properties of circulating capital for properties of things such as raw materials or wage-provisions, or the properties of fixed capital for those of things such as machinery in which capital is materialised. Marx criticises the political economists, using terms from 'the thing and its properties':

> The crude materialism of the economists, who regard social relations of production among people, and determinations which pertain to objects that capitalists are concerned with [*Sachen*], as they are subsumed under these relations, as *natural properties* of things [*natürliche Eigenschaften der Dinge*], is likewise a crude idealism, even fetishism, which imputes social relations to things as immanent determinations, and thus mystifies them (N 687, M 567; quotation largely altered).

For example, in the *Grundrisse* machinery is circulating capital so long as it circulates as commodities. In that way it is potential fixed capital in circulation. However, political economists, such as Ricardo, distinguish between circulating and fixed capital according to the natural, physical properties inherent in them, the physical properties in which the value of capital has been incarnated. Ricardo ascribes an annual return from capital, e.g. profit or interest, to natural properties of things by analogy with a tree bearing fruit. Marx writes:

> Capital itself as *processing* — hence, as accomplishing one turnover — is regarded as *working capital*, and the fruits [e.g. profit or interest], which it is supposed to yield, are calculated according to its working time — the total circulation time of one turnover. The mystification which thereby takes place lies in the nature of capital (N 640, M 525; quotation partially altered).

Economists are obsessed with a crude materialism, because unawares they mistake properties inherent in the value-relation or capital-relation for properties of material things, and in that way they misunderstand the materialisation of capitalist 'concern' (*Sache*). They are also afflicted with a crude idealism, because they do not notice that the value-relation and capital-relation, which are both ideal *par excellence* and are alienated mediations of the power of thought (*telos*), are materialised in material things. Instead they presume that a thing in itself, e.g. gold, is the origin of an ideal property, e.g. value. Thus Marx demonstrates that capitalist value-consciousness is inherent in the turnover of productive capital, and then he shows how it is transformed into a consciousness that is permeated with crude materialism and with idealism.

For Marx materialism is never understood in terms of reflection theory, as found in Stalinist Marxism. Rather it signifies that human beings arise from nature, and in that way nature is their *mater* (mother), or 'matter'; human beings must also derive a living from nature or 'matter'. Marx's 'material-ism' indicates that humans have a substantial dependence on nature or matter, and in other words, it is a 'naturalism' associated with the 'humanism' manifested in the *Economic and philosophical manuscripts (1844)*.

Moreover in the pre-history of modern society the material life that humans must engage in takes on alienated forms in history. In spite of alienation, however, a process of social development gradually prepares a real possibility for human emancipation. Alienation in class society, typically value-relations and capital-relations, rules and develops the material forces of nature itself and the powers of human nature. This proceeds to an extreme point at which alienation ceases to exist. Therefore Marx's materialism has another sense, in that historical forms predominate over natural 'matter', such as human beings and nature itself. But in his view the formal structures through which this predominance is exercised are destined for collapse.

The conversion of the law of appropriation and 'causality'

Marx again discusses the conversion of the law of appropriation, this time with respect to his division of 'the whole process' of capital-circulation into 'small-scale circulation' and 'large-scale circulation'. Through the exchange of capital with labour-power in small-scale circulation, capital absorbs the surplus product and realises it as surplus-value. When this circuit of money-capital is repeated at least twice, the law of exchange of equivalents becomes merely formal, because a non-equivalent is appropriated, namely surplus-value.

In explaining the conversion of the law of appropriation at the end of his discussion of 'generality of capital', Marx refers to Hegel's 'absolute necessity'. Here (N 673–8, M 555–9), however, the conversion is linked to Hegel's 'causality or reciprocity between cause and effect', which follows 'absolute necessity' in his *Logic*.

For Marx the use-value of a commodity functions as 'cause', because the means of consumption reproduces human life, and the means of production is consumed in order to provide new products. The specific use-value of labour-power is the cause of the valorisation of capital, because only labour-power can create the new value from which surplus-value is ultimately derived. By contrast, he considers the exchange-value of a commodity as 'effect', because of its relationship to use-value as 'cause'.

> In this exchange [between capital and labour], then, the labourer receives the equivalent of the labour-time objectified in him, and gives his value-creating, value-increasing living labour-time. He sells himself as effect [*Effect*]. As cause [*Ursache*], as activity he is absorbed and incarnated [*incarniert*] in capital. Thus the exchange converts into its opposite, and the laws of private property — liberty, equality, property — property in one's own labour, and free disposition over it — convert into the labourer's propertylessness and exteriorization [*Entäusserung*] of his labour, into his relation to it as alien property and vice versa (N 674, M 556; quotation largely altered).

In his consideration of capitalist production as a dynamic system, Marx does not apply a one-sided causality, moving simply from cause to effect. Instead he uses an organic causality, e.g. in his discussion of the process of reproduction of an economic system. This is a kind of causality captured by Hegel in his *Logic*, where effect turns into cause as a process proceeds from one phase to the next. Because of the labourer's propertylessness or alienation from the product of labour, the labourer is once again forced to work and to reproduce this propertylessness, which appears as the capitalist's appropriation of unpaid labour.

However, Marx does not repeat his discussion of the conversion of the law of appropriation, but redefines his view by including in it the concrete form of provision for the labourer in terms of circulating capital:

> The labourer's *approvisionnement* arises out of the production process, as product, as result; but it never enters as such into the production process, because it is a finished product for

> individual consumption, enters immediately into the labourer's consumption, and is immediately exchanged for it. This, therefore, as distinct from raw material as well as instrument, is the circulating capital *par excellence* (N 675, M 556; quotation partially altered).[6]

Here Marx's description advances to the reproduction of the relation between capital and labour (N 676–8, M 557–9), because he relates the conversion of the law of appropriation to Hegel's 'reciprocity between cause and effect'. But once again he divides the whole process into small-scale and large-scale circulation. This precedes his consideration of the turnover of capital (N 618–721, M 505–97). Then he takes up the process of reproduction through circulation, i.e. the determination of fixed and circulating capital as 'individuality'. Therefore his treatment of the conversion of the law of appropriation with reference to Hegel's 'causality' is properly considered as part of the discussion of reproduction through circulation (N 721–43, M 597–616).

The individual determination and 'the disjunctive judgement'

Marx now advances to the third determination 'individuality', in which he clarifies the process of reproduction for one capital[7] through simple circulation in which use-value is merely replaced:

> Since we speak here of capital *as such* [*das Kapital*], capital in the process of becoming [*das werdende Kapital*], we are not yet concerned with anything else in addition — in that the many capitals are not yet present for us — nothing but it itself and simple circulation [*es selbst* (= *das Kapital in allgemeinen*) *und die einfache Circulation* — *sic*] . . . (N 729, M 605).

Marx touches on the relation between 'capital in general' and simple circulation when he again considers the determination 'generality':

> As commodity, capital throws itself out of its own circulation into general circulation; and, again as commodity, capital leaves general circulation and enters its own course, issuing into the production process. The circulation of capital thus

> contains a relation to general circulation, of which its own circulation forms a moment, while the latter likewise appears as posited by capital. This to be examined later (N 619–20, M 506).

'This to be examined later' refers to Marx's consideration of the reproduction process of one capital through simple circulation, which occurs in the discussion of 'particularizing capital' in the *Grundrisse*.

Firstly, the product of capital (commodity-capital or C′) is defined as circulating capital. In circulating capital, through the twofold character of labour, circulating variable capital (V) is wholly reproduced, surplus-value (S) is created, and the whole circulating constant capital (C_c) and a part of fixed constant capital (C_f) are preserved, so $C' = V + S + C_c + C_f$. In large-scale circulation the commodity as circulating capital is sold and transformed into money as circulating capital, so $C' - M'$.

Secondly, capital purchases the objective and subjective conditions of its reproduction in the same process of circulation where $M - C(L_p + P_m)$. Following Smith, Marx presupposes that one capital as 'subject' in bourgeois society produces its means of consumption and is supplied with them through large-scale circulation. In that process of simple circulation it purchases:

1. the means of production, which consist of raw material as circulating capital, considered as the product of an abstract producer supplied with provisions and raw materials from circulating capital;
2. the means of labour, especially machinery which has also been produced and sold in the same way as raw materials; machinery is sold as circulating capital, and it becomes fixed capital *in actu* in the production process.

Labour-power is sold in the course of small-scale circulation, and it is reproduced through individual consumption of the means for life; in large-scale circulation it is sold as circulating capital. The capitalist obtains a portion of surplus-value as a fund for individual life, and the capitalist purchases the means of consumption for self-renewal as the mediator for capital.

One capital thus reproduces its own value and use-value as well as the capital–labour relationship; this happens in the forms of circulating and fixed capital. What should not be overlooked here is the fact that both circulating and fixed capital, into which one capital particularises itself, are transformed into value and use-value in the process of reproduction through circulation, yet the differences between circulating and fixed capital are preserved.

This process by which capital is reproduced through circulation incorporates a reciprocity such that fixed capital, e.g. machinery, is produced with circulating capital, e.g. provisions and raw materials, and circulating capital itself is then reproduced through the use of fixed capital.

> . . . although circulating capital and fixed capital now appear as two different sorts [*2 verschiedne Arten*], circulating capital is still posited through the consumption, the wear of fixed capital; while fixed capital, for its part, exists only as circulating capital transformed into this determinate form (N 738, M 612; quotation partially altered).

Because the determination of capital as such comes from circulation, capital as the 'notion' starts off in the form of money as potential capital. The substantial form of this potential capital is circulating capital. Provisions and raw materials must take the form of circulating capital, and so does machinery:

> Assuming the process of production of capital: *All capital returns only in the form of a circulating capital*; hence fixed capital can be renewed only by a process in which a part of circulating capital becomes fixed; hence, by the employment of part of the raw materials produced, and a part of labour consumed (hence also a part of the *approvisionnement* exchanged for living labour) for the production of fixed capital (N 734, M 609).

The two sorts of capital — circulating and fixed — into which one capital is particularised, have once again become one capital or 'individuality' through a reciprocal transformation between them in terms of value and use-value. Marx's view on the mediation of use-value by value, introduced at the beginning of the 'Chapter on Capital', is thus in continuous use up to this point. Capital now appears in the determinate form of circulating capital as a whole, maintaining particular moments of the two sorts of capital — circulating and fixed — within itself, so the positive aspect of 'generality' emerges once again, and 'all capital is circulating capital'. 'Individuality' as the unity of 'generality' and 'particularity', as traced in Hegel's 'disjunctive judgement', is applied by Marx to the reproduction of one capital through simple circulation:

> If, in this exteriorization [*Entäusserung*] of the notion, its inner identity is at the same time *posited*, the general is the genus [*Gattung*] which is self-identical in its exclusive individuality. This judgement, which has this general for both its terms, the one time as general, the other time as the circle of its self-excluding particularization in which *Either–Or* as much as *As Well As* is the genus, is the *Disjunctive Judgement*. Generality, at first as genus [*Gattung*], and now also as the circuit of its species [*Arten*], is thus determined as posited as totality (sect. 177; quotation largely altered).[8]

Through its differentiation into *either* circulating capital *or* fixed capital, one capital is now united as individuality, a state in which it is circulating capital *as well as* fixed capital. The differences between them are still preserved in this process of reproduction through circulation. In the process of 'particularization', one capital becomes 'individuality' in the form of circulating capital as a whole. This is an individuality that is unified as a totality, including the particularising moments preserved within it. This 'disjunctive judgement' is most in evidence when Marx grasps the process of reproduction of one capital through simple circulation.

Second critique of Hegel's system

Thus far one capital has re-emerged from circulation as one capital or a totality, in which circulating and fixed capital once again exclude each other. But this is no longer a simple whole (*ein blosses Ganze*) of money-capital, as it is at the beginning of Marx's consideration of the 'generality of capital'. 'Money as capital' has first become the general notion of capital, and then capital as the general notion begins to particularise itself as two kinds of capital — circulating and fixed — according to the specific material moment in which the value of capital is mediated. At the peak of its particularisation, the two kinds of capital are transformed into each other, so the process of reproduction of one capital then forms a complex structure as one totality (*eine Totalität*) with particular determinations preserved. Marx's method in constructing a critique of political economy, defined in his Introduction to the *Grundrisse*, is one of appropriating the concrete, in order to reproduce theoretically the structure of bourgeois society in which capital is dominant.

This process of becoming (*werden*) one totality is presupposed logically and historically by Marx. At the beginning of his consideration of the 'generality of capital', Marx refers to Hegel's 'positing reflection' in order to clarify the reciprocal relationship between presupposition and positing in the bourgeois economic system as it reproduces itself. He then adds that the system has historical presuppositions which were posited in the past. Therefore the historical origination of capitalism is described after he considers the accumulation of capital, and it forms a criterion for determining which basic conditions are required for capitalism. This analysis is carried out in the section of the *Grundrisse* known as 'Pre-capitalist economic formations'.

This analysis implies a critique of Hegel's view of circular systems as closed. Marx demonstrates that capitalism is an open system with respect to the past, because its conditions of existence were posited in a pre-capitalist period. But with his theory of 'disposable time', he also predicts that capitalism contains within itself a possibility that it will cease to exist in future. Thus he shows that capitalism is a historical phenomenon that is open with respect to both past and future.

At the end of Marx's discussion of 'particularity of capital', he confirms that the exchange between capital and labour is indispensable to capital-accumulation, and he inquires further how free labourers came to exist in the past. Those labourers are 'free' in a twofold sense, in that they are citizens with equal rights in modern society, and they are also free, i.e. alienated from the means of production which remain the property of others. Quoting from Sir Frederick Morton Eden's *The state of the poor, or an history of the labouring classes in England from the Conquest etc.*, Marx points out that civilised institutions guarantee the right for a small number of non-labourers to appropriate products made by workers, leaving some of their labour unpaid:

> Our zone requires labour for the satisfaction of needs, and *therefore* at least *one part* of society must *always tirelessly* labour; others labour in the arts etc., and some, who do not work, still have the products of diligence at their disposal. For this, these proprietors have only *civilization and order* to thank; they

are purely the creatures of *civilized institutions* (N 735, M 610).

Marx also notes that the 'bloody legislation' of Henry VII, Henry VIII, Edward VI and Elizabeth I *de facto* forced peasants to become wage-labourers for capitalists. But he also recognises that 'disposable time' is a potential within surplus-value as produced by capitalism, and that this potential develops further as fixed capital increases. This disposable time corresponds as a potential to the development of workers' organisations, and he forecasts that they will become aware of their own abilities and powers, which have for so long been appropriated by capitalists. In that way he describes a phenomenology of mind or spirit that develops towards human freedom.

> *The creation of a large quantity of disposable time* apart from necessary labour-time for society generally and each of its members (i.e. room for the development of the individuals' full productive forces, hence those of society also), this creation of non-labour-time appears in the stage of capital, as of all earlier ones, as non-labour-time, free time, for a few. What capital adds is that it increases the surplus-labour-time of the mass by all the means of art and science, because its wealth consists directly in the appropriation of surplus-labour-time; since *value directly is its purpose*, not use-value. It is thus, despite itself, instrumental in creating the means of social disposable time, in order to reduce labour-time for the whole society to a diminishing minimum, and thus to free everyone's time for their own development. But its tendency always, on the one side, [is] *to create disposable time, on the other, to convert it into surplus-labour* . . . The more this contradiction develops, the more does it become evident that the growth of the forces of production can no longer be bound up with the appropriation of alien labour, but that the mass of labourers must themselves appropriate their own surplus-labour. Once they have done so — and *disposable time* thereby ceases to have an *opposite* existence . . . (N 708, M 583–4; quotation partially altered).

The way in which disposable time is removed from the hands of capitalists and freed for the enjoyment of workers is demonstrated theoretically as follows. In capitalism workers are separated from the products of their labour, which include the means of production and the means of consumption. Those products are produced from 'matter' by their own labour as 'form'. Their alienation from the products of their own labour amounts to an indefensible separation from 'matter' or nature, which is vital to human life. Because of their alienation from 'matter' (*hylē*), and because of their pressing need for the means of life, they must alienate their own labour-power once again to the capitalist, who holds exclusive sway over the means of production. By virtue of this, the capitalist controls production as the mediator for capital and so monopolises mental labour. The capitalist forces workers to engage in physical labour, and this alienation from 'matter' causes an alienation from labour as 'form' (*telos*).

The universal truth that human beings arise from the natural world and cannot live without material contact with nature is deformed under capitalism, because capitalists have exclusive ownership of 'matter' as land and the products of labour. Desperate for the means of subsistence, wage-labourers must alienate their labour-power by the hour, and they become obedient to capitalist command.

This relationship between capitalist and labourer can be expressed in terms of Aristotle's theory of 'cause' as follows. 'Final cause' (*telos*) for labourers is a representation in advance of the end-product of their activity. This is alienated to the capitalist. The labourer obtains 'material cause' (*hylē*) as the means of consumption and engages in labour that is merely physical. This is 'efficient cause' (*archē*) under capitalist control. The capitalist has exclusive ownership over the means of production or 'material cause' (*hylē*), and then takes on the task of mental labour as 'final cause' (*telos*). This is not the same 'final cause' as occurs in the labour-process, but is rather an alienated, abstract practice that pursues an increase in the value of capital through identifying and manipulating its various shapes. In that way Aristotle's four causes are linked within the production-process of capital, pursued through the relation of commodity-exchange.

Because there is a motive for obtaining surplus-profit, each individual capitalist manages and controls the production-process at the micro-level through rational planning. Capitalist practice at that level is 'final cause'. On the macro-level, however, the practice of capitalists considered as a whole becomes 'efficient cause',[9] and this brings two unexpected effects: relative surplus-value, and a decrease in the general rate of profit. Each capitalist aims to reduce the value of each individual product in order to obtain a margin between socially established value and the value of an individual product, thus obtaining a surplus-profit, for which capitalists compete with each other. To obtain this margin, capitalists introduce machinery in order to increase the productivity of labour, and so the value of an individual product decreases. This innovative aspect of competition transforms the process of production into a scientific process of industrial development. It also pushes individual labourers to realise their collective power in terms of scientific knowledge. The capitalist must educate the labourer as manager and controller of this scientific production-process, so a process of education, which is initially in the interest of the capitalist, paradoxically realises some of the labourer's potential power. This change occurs in the development of the means of production which proceeds from tools, used by skilled labourers, up to machinery, in which human skills are overtaken by a scientific analysis of production as a mechanised process. Skilled physical labour is then replaced by machinery, which is the power of science made manifest. In Aristotle's terms 'efficient cause' in the productive process is no longer human hands but machinery. Marx writes:

> No longer does the labourer insert a modified natural object as middle link between the object and himself; rather, he inserts the process of nature [*Naturprocess*] which he transforms into an industrial process, as means between himself and inorganic nature, mastering it. He steps to the side of the production process instead of being its main agency [*Hauptagent*]. In this transformation, it is neither the direct human labour he himself performs, nor the time during which he works, but rather the appropriation of his own general productive force, his understanding of nature and his mastery over it through his existence [*Dasein*] as social body [*Gesellschaftskörper*] — it is, in a word, the development of the social individual which appears as the great foundation-stone of production and of wealth. The *theft of alien labour-time, on which the present wealth is based*, appears a miserable foundation in the face of this new one, created by large-scale industry itself (N 705, M 581; quotation partially altered).
>
> It [fixed capital] . . . [now] exists merely as agency [*Agent*] for the transformation of the raw material into the product (N 691, M 570).
>
> . . . to the degree that large industry develops, the creation of real wealth comes to depend less on labour-time and on the

> amount of labour employed than on the power of the agencies [*die Macht der Agentien*] set in motion during labour-time, whose powerful effectiveness is itself in turn out of all proportion to the direct labour-time spent on their production, but depends rather on the general state of science and on the progress of technology, or the application of this science to production (N 704–5, M 581).

In the production process 'efficient cause' or 'agent' is thus transformed from physical labour into machinery. At the same time, the labourer, rather than the capitalist, takes on the role of 'final cause'. The labourer changes from 'efficient cause' (*archē*) to 'final cause' (*telos*), and tools are converted from 'material cause' (*hylē*) into machinery or 'efficient cause'. Simultaneously physical labour as 'efficient cause' becomes mental labour or 'final cause'. The main 'efficient cause' of the capitalist production-process changes from skilled labour or 'living labour' to automatic machinery or 'dead labour'.

This transition suggests that 'living labour', which has hitherto been the 'general substance' of capital and the mediator in reproducing the material and subjective conditions of the capital-relation, now begins to vanish from the production-process. This means that capitalist development tends to let the substance of value diminish almost to zero, and so it destroys its own basis:

> . . . the value objectified in machinery appears as a presupposition against which the value-creating force of the individual labour-power is an infinitesimal vanishing magnitude [*als ein unendlich kleines verschwindet*] . . . (N 694, M 573; quotation partially altered).

While the productivity of labour increases without limit, 'living labour' or V + S added to the product tends to diminish almost to zero. At the same time, the durability of machinery improves, so fixed constant capital, which is transferred to and preserved in the product, diminishes, and circulating constant capital cheapens, because of the increased productivity of labour. In that way the value of the product or C + V + S decreases. Paradoxically each capitalist's capacity for innovation, which derives from striving for surplus-profit, causes the law of value to collapse, and hence the capitalist mode of production. After that there is no capital, and therefore no capitalist or wage-labourer. Instead there are free workers, who organise themselves in a scientific system of production. They manage and control the system in accordance with high standards, so they are now free 'subjects' in social production, regaining their own 'final cause' (*telos*). Surplus-labour-time, extended under capitalist production, then becomes available for workers to apportion into material funds for social investment and 'disposable time' for individual and social development.

In history so far producers have been alienated from their 'final cause' and forced to labour as an 'efficient cause' through the capital-relation. But in Marx's view, human beings arose with the two causes united. It is because of the profit motive that capitalism develops their mental abilities ('final cause') through an educational system and network of communication. At last they can recover this 'final cause' in a highly advanced form. What nature has given to human beings ('final cause') can be separated from them by human action in society, but this 'final cause' can be regained, and Marx includes these notions in his materialism.

As explained above, 'efficient cause' as physical ability is, so to speak, 'material cause' in relation to 'final cause' as mental ability. Mental ability is 'formal cause' (*eidos*) as such, which is generated on the basis of 'material cause' in the human body. 'Efficient cause' can be temporarily suspended within social relations, but in Marx's account it is destined to be reunited with its original 'material cause' and 'final cause' after its cultivation through the historical development of alienated societies. The mental ability of the wage-labourer undergoes a developmental process through alienation in capitalist society. This may be called Marx's phenomenology of mind, which he develops from Hegel's *Phenomenology*, and it is applied to the critique of political economy.

For Marx the human being arises from a 'material cause' as such (*natura naturans*), develops as a 'formal cause', which re-forms 'matter' (nature) and develops human nature itself. Marx's materialism is associated with a view that human alienation as 'formal cause' is destined to be transcended through its own development.[10] The purpose of Marx's critique of political economy is, *inter alia*, to demonstrate the validity of his materialism. In the *Grundrisse* he begins for the first time to carry out this task systematically.

5

The 'Chapter on Capital' and the Doctrine of Essence, Part Three: 'Individuality of Capital'

Profit and 'syllogism'

In 'I. Generality of Capital' Marx considers the development or 'becoming' (*werden*) of the 'notion' of capital. And in 'II. Particularity of Capital' he traces one capital, as representative of the 'notion', to its differentiation into two kinds of capital. He does this with reference to 'the judgement' as outlined in Hegel's *Logic*. In the final section 'III. Individuality of Capital' of his triadic structure, Marx grasps capital as a totality or 'individuality', with reference to Hegel's 'syllogism'.

At the conclusion of 'II. Particularity of Capital', Marx establishes the division of capital into two kinds — fixed and circulating. Those two kinds of capital undergo mutual transformations in simple circulation within the reproduction process of one capital. The complex structure of this totality corresponds to Hegel's 'disjunctive judgement'.

However, as Hegel explains: 'This disruption of the notion, posited by its proper activity in differentiating its moments, is the *judgement*, the significance of which after this must be comprehended as the *particularizing* of the notion' (sect. 166, Z; quotation largely altered).[1] The real content of the disjunctive judgement is something more than that of the judgement as such, since it demonstrates that the 'general' becomes the 'individual' through its extreme 'particularization'. For Hegel this constitutes the 'syllogism':

> . . . the actual is an *individual*, which, through the *particularity*, raises itself to the *generality* and makes itself identical with

> itself. — The actual is one [*Eines*], but it is also the divergence from each other of the moments of the notion, and the Syllogism is the circulation of the intermediation of its moments, through which it posits itself as one [*Eines*] (sect. 181; quotation largely altered).

Hegel's syllogism consists of 'qualitative syllogism', 'syllogism of reflection' and 'syllogism of necessity'. The form in which the 'general' becomes an 'individual' through 'particularization' is the final syllogism of 'necessity', equivalent to the disjunctive judgement. The two are equivalent because Hegel defines the disjunctive judgement as 'the circle of its self-excluding particularization' (sect. 177), and the syllogism of necessity as the 'totality of its *particularizings* [*Totalität seiner Besonderungen*] [of the general]' (sect. 191; quotation partially altered).

Marx considers the reproduction process of capital at the conclusion of 'II. Particularity of Capital', and he treats profit in 'III. Individuality of Capital'. This order corresponds to the relation between the 'judgement' and the 'syllogism' in Hegel's *Logic*. The process of reproduction is located in both sections II and III, and this corresponds to the equivalence of 'judgement' and 'syllogism'.

This syllogistic mode of thinking, in which actuality is understood as a self-reproducing organic structure, is common to the *Grundrisse* and to Smith's *The wealth of nations*.[2] Smith's theory of reproduction is contained in the chapters in Book I on the division of labour and in Book II on investment. Moreover each chapter of Book II is described as reproduction theory. It is notable that Smith considers not only the material conditions of reproduction, but also profit and interest in relation to reproduction in Book II, so the structure of Smith's theory can be seen in Marx's work in the *Grundrisse*. Marx develops the reproduction process at the end of 'II. Particularity of Capital', where he investigates the material conditions of reproduction, citing Smith. And in the course of 'III. Individuality of Capital' he treats profit in relation to the reproduction of capital. The *Grundrisse* has a syllogistic structure and an economic content which shows Marx's appropriation of both classic authors, Hegel and Smith.

Profit of capital and 'positing reflection, ground, identity and difference'

Marx begins his discussion of 'III. Individuality of Capital' or 'capital as fructiferous' as follows:

> Capital is now posited as the unity of production and circulation . . . Capital is now realized not only as value which reproduces itself and is hence perennial, but also as value which posits value. Through the absorption of living labour-time and through the movement of its own circulation . . . it relates to itself as positing new value, as producer of value. It relates as the ground [*Grund*] to surplus-value, something grounded [*Begründete*] by it. Its movement consists of relating to itself, while it produces itself, as the ground of itself at the same time as what is grounded, as value presupposed to itself as surplus-value, or [value presupposed] to surplus-value as posited by it (N 745, M 619; quotation partially altered).

As demonstrated above, Marx defines the relation between capital and surplus-value with reference to Hegel's 'positing reflection' and 'ground'. Here capital has posited itself as one totality, and it has established itself as value that ceaselessly produces new value, making the various moments of production and circulation into factors which create values. Capital appears as self-increasing value. However, value itself is the accumulation of surplus-value extracted from an exploited wage-labourer through the conversion of the law of appropriation. In other words, the presuppositions of capital are what capital itself has posited. This confirms that 'positing reflection', here referred to by Marx for the third time, clarifies the reciprocity between presupposition and positing.

In the passage from the *Grundrisse* cited above, there is another reference to Hegel's *Logic*. As mentioned at the beginning of the 'Chapter on Capital', the contradiction within the third determination of money — money as treasure or 'money as money' — dissolves itself into 'ground' (*Grund*), i.e. production. This is *de facto* the production of commodities structured by capital at the point where commodities are produced for simple circulation.

However, the capitalist does not aim at producing use-value

itself, but at obtaining surplus-value, the 'form as content' of value. Following the realisation of this 'form as content', Marx redefines 'ground', not as simple commodity-production, but as 'ground' in relation to capital and surplus-value.

Because surplus-value is posited by capital, capital is the 'ground' of surplus-value, and surplus-value is what is 'grounded' by capital. Hegel describes 'ground' and 'the grounded':

> The *determinateness* of essence as ground is herewith twofold, that of the *ground* and the *grounded*. It is, first, essence as ground, *determined* as essence over against positedness, determined, that is as a *non-positedness*. Secondly, it is the grounded, the immediate, which however is not in and for itself; it is posited *qua* positedness.[3]

The relation between 'ground' and 'the grounded' continues, because capital identifies itself as such through positing surplus-value, so capital is 'grounded' by surplus-value, and surplus-value is the 'ground' of capital. The 'ground' of surplus-value, which 'grounds' capital, is capital itself. The reciprocity between 'ground' and 'the grounded' is further developed in the transformation of surplus-value into capital. Surplus-value becomes capital. Thus surplus-value 'grounded' by capital changes into capital, its 'ground', and now posits surplus-value. Surplus-capital posits surplus-value, or surplus-capital 'grounds' surplus-value. Capital is thus transformed by surplus-value, and the relation between capital and surplus-value is one of identity.

Hegel continues his exposition with a discussion of 'self-identity':

> This, therefore, is likewise self-identical, but is the identity of the negative with itself. The self-identical negative and the self-identical positve are *now one and the same identity*. For the ground is the identity of the positive or even of positedness, too, with itself; the grounded is positedness *qua* positedness, but this its reflection-into-self is the identity of the ground.[4]

'Ground' at the beginning of 'I. Generality of Capital' refers simply to commodity-production. There the contradiction within money in its third determination — money as treasure or 'money as money' — dissolves itself, and capital posits surplus-value. However, here both 'ground' and 'the grounded' illustrate the relation between capital and surplus-value. Marx defines profit as a relation within surplus-value itself:

> — capital relates to itself as self-increasing value; i.e. it relates to surplus-value as something posited and grounded by it; it relates as well-spring [*Quelle*] of production [of surplus-value], to itself as product [of surplus-value]; it relates to itself as producing [surplus] value, as produced [surplus] value. It therefore no longer measures the newly produced [surplus] value by its real measure, the relation of surplus-labour to necessary labour, but rather by itself as its presupposition. One capital [*ein Kapital*] of a certain value produces in a certain period of time a certain surplus-value. Surplus-value is thus measured by the value of the presupposed capital, capital thus posited as self-realizing value — is *profit* (N 746, M 620; quotation partially altered).

Surplus-value is no longer measured with respect to variable capital, because capital is manifested as surplus-value accumulated and transformed. Capital is now measured as a whole, i.e. the whole surplus-value as accumulated value, because what has just been posited is identical with what has already been posited. Surplus-value as a presupposition is the same as surplus-value accumulated in the past; it is now shown to be no different from new surplus-value. New surplus-value is consequently measured within capital in the same way as old surplus-value. Marx thus redefines surplus-value as profit:

> After it has distinguished the profit, as newly reproduced value, from itself as presupposed, self-realizing value, and has posited profit as the measure of its realization [*Verwertung*], it transcends the separation [i.e. transforms profit into capital] again, and posits it in its identity [*Identität*] to itself as capital which, grown by the amount of the profit, now begins the same process anew in larger dimensions (N 746, M 620; quotation partially altered).

At the beginning of 'I. Generality of Capital', where Marx starts to explain the transition from money to capital, he refers to 'identity' and 'difference'. He does this to define capital as it exists in the sphere of circulation. Capital is the 'identity' of value which persists through the mediation by the capitalist of various 'differences' in its metamorphoses. Marx uses these two terms — 'identity' and 'difference' — in his initial definition of capital. Here he uses them to help grasp the relation between capital and surplus-value when he redefines it as profit.

Productive capital and 'the whole and its parts', 'force and its manifestation'

Marx then defines capital as 'the equally productive', referring again to Hegel's 'the whole and its part' and 'force and its manifestation':

> *While capital is posited as profit-positing, as a source of wealth independently of labour, each part [Teil] of the capital is thereby assumed to be equally productive [gleichmässig productiv].* Just as surplus-value in the form of profit is measured against the whole value [*Gesamtwert*] of the capital, so does it appear to be created equally by its different component parts [*Bestandteile*]. Thus its circulating part [*Teil*] . . . brings no more profit than the component part which forms the fixed capital; that is, profit relates equally [*gleichmässig*] to these component parts in proportion to their magnitude (N 759–60, M 632; quotation partially altered).

Since capital has become 'one totality', each part of capital appears equally productive as a profit-producing factor of production. Labour no longer appears as the source of profit, and the productive forces of labour are perversely 'manifested' as the 'force' of capital. The whole of capital, not merely a particular part, appears as 'fructiferous'. Here again Marx is evidently thinking of Hegel's 'force and its manifestation'.

In the valorisation process, as Marx presents it in 'I. Generality of Capital', he connects Hegel's terms with the relation between the component parts of capital-value — constant capital and variable capital — and the resultant surplus-value. Here, however, Marx incorporates his analysis from 'II. Particularity of Capital', demonstrating that the productive forces of social labour — collective and scientific — appear as properties of circulating and fixed capital. He then demonstrates that circulation-time, as well as production-time, appear as equally productive with respect to the generation of profit. All the moments of capital are now 'manifest' as factors of the 'force' of capital.

Marx's use of 'force and its manifestation' is linked with his use of 'the whole and its parts' mentioned above. Since every component part of capital appears to be equally productive, the whole capital-value does not appear to be divided into various parts, but united into one totality. The value of capital appears as 'a simple whole' (*ein blosses Ganze*) at the transition of money to capital, but now seems to have become 'a determinate totality' (*ein bestimmte Totalität*)[5] for us (*für uns*), who have followed all the movements of capital after the transition. As capital appears to be 'one', so profit appears to be what each part of capital equally has brought about. Thus the component parts of capital disappear and capital appears as 'one'.

As already demonstrated, Hegel mistakes the 'whole' for 'content', and 'parts' for 'forms', but Marx suggests in the valorisation process that the 'whole' is the 'form' of capital and the 'parts' are its 'content' or use-value. And he clarifies this for the turnover of capital in 'II. Particularity of Capital', so that the 'whole' is also its 'form' and the 'parts' are its 'content'. In that 'content' the 'form' or value of capital is mediated, and capital divides into two kinds — circulating and fixed. Here in Marx's discussion of profit in 'III. Individuality of Capital', the two kinds of capital are transformed into each other in order to become 'one determinate totality', so capital returns to 'one' and relates to surplus-value as profit:

> Since capital enters wholly (*ganz*) into production, and since, as capital, its various component parts are only formally distinct from one another, are equally sums of value, it follows that the positing of value appears to be equally inherent in them. Furthermore, since the part of the capital which exchanges for labour acts productively *only in so far as the other parts of capital are posited together with it* — and since the relation of this productivity is conditioned by the magnitude of the value etc., the various relations of these parts to one another (as fixed capital etc.) — it follows that the positing of surplus-value, of profit, appears to be determined by all parts of capital equally (N 822, M 685–6).

In that way Marx demonstrates the reason why surplus-value is determined as profit. This is because capital has become 'equally productive' or 'one determinate totality', and he has further shown that capital and surplus-value stand in a twofold relation to each other based on 'ground' and 'the grounded' — capital is 'grounded' by surplus-value, the 'ground' for which is capital; and surplus-value, 'grounded' by capital, becomes capital, its 'ground'.

Form of production and form of distribution, and 'causality'

Marx's next task is to trace the transformation of profit:

> The product of capital, thus, is profit. By relating to itself as profit, it relates to itself as the *source of the production of value, and the rate of profit expresses the proportion by which it has increased its own value.* But the capitalist is not merely capital. He has to live, and since he does not live by labour, he must live on profit, i.e. on the alien labour he appropriates. Thus capital is posited as the source of wealth. Since it has incorporated productivity into itself as its immanent attribute, capital relates to profit as *revenue* (N 758, M 630; quotation partially altered).

Surplus-value is now determined not only as profit but also as revenue. However, Marx has not yet distinguished between the revenue of capital itself and revenue as the fund for maintaining the capitalist as an individual. As defined above, revenue is part of profit, which is distributed to the capitalist as a fund for subsistence. Profit is now divided into individual revenue for the capitalist and the fund for capital accumulation. For the conversion of the law of appropriation, all surplus-value was presumed to be in transformation to surplus-capital, and there it was shown that the more surplus-value is transformed into capital, the less 'original non-surplus capital' remains. It gradually diminishes to a *magnitudo evanescens*.[6]

In the reproduction process considered at the end of 'II. Particularity of Capital', use-value itself is replaced through circulation, so it is now theoretically possible to divide profit into funds for capital accumulation and funds for maintaining the capitalist as an individual. Then the original capital, presumed to contain no surplus-value, is paid out from time to time for subsistence. But over time it is replaced by surplus-value. In that way the capitalist's original fund is not independent — as political economists sometimes claimed — of the surplus-value generated by labourers.

From the labourer's standpoint, variable capital is a wage-fund for maintaining the labourer's life, so a part of profit is revenue for the capitalist. Therefore the conditions for reproduction are now posited not only in objective but in subjective terms:

> Thus profit appears as a *form of distribution*, like wages. But since capital can grow only through the retransformation of profit into capital — into surplus-capital — profit is at the same time a *form of production for capital*; just exactly as wages are a mere *relation of production* from the standpoint of capital, a relation of distribution from the labourer's standpoint. This shows that the relations of distribution are themselves produced by the relations of production, and represent the latter themselves from another point of view. It shows further that the relation of production to consumption is posited by production itself (N 758, M 631).

Profit as revenue, i.e. a fund for maintaining the capitalist, is a form of distribution. Profit, however, is a form of production from the viewpoint of the capitalist, since, on the one hand, it reproduces the capitalist as the mediator of capital, and, on the other hand, it is transformed into surplus-capital. The situation is the same with wages. Though wages appear as a form of distribution for the labourer, they are also a form of production for the capitalist, who organises and manages production, and under whom the labourer is subsumed as the actual mediator of capital through the twofold character of labour — creator of new values and preserver of old. As we have previously seen in the Introduction to the *Grundrisse*, forms of distribution are linked to forms of production through the reproduction process, which includes productive consumption and individual consumption for subsistence.

Forms of distribution, such as profit and wages, are results of the production of capital, and they become presuppositions for the next round in production:

> While profit thus appears in one respect as the result of capital, it appears in the other as the *presupposition of capital formation*. Thus is posited anew the circular movement in

which the result appears as presupposition (N 759, M 631).

This circular relation between result and presupposition, or effect and cause, is based on Hegel's 'relationship of causality' in the *Logic*: '. . . according to its identity with the cause itself, the effect is defined as cause, and at the same time as an *other* cause, which again has another effect, and so on for ever (sect. 153; quotation largely altered).

The causal relation in which 'effect' in the form of distribution appears as a presupposition in the form of production, is similar to the relation 'causality' described by Hegel above.[7] In Marx's discussion of reproduction at the end of 'I. Generality of Capital' he clarifies the accumulation of value and the reproduction of capital. In discussing reproduction again at the end of 'II. Particularity of Capital', he considers the process of accumulation of value and the replacement of use-value. Here at the end of 'III. Individuality of Capital' he demonstrates not only the reproduction of objects but also the reproduction of subjects within the capital-relation, as production and distribution are reciprocal.

Third critique of Hegel's system

At the end of 'III. Individuality of Capital' Marx again criticises Hegel's circular system, because it reflects capitalism in abstract terms. He argues that Hegel's closed, logical system is actually historical — it has an origin in the past and will vanish in future — so it is open in both directions. He accomplishes this task by using his theories of primitive accumulation and 'disposable time'.

In discussing the accumulation of capital at the end of 'I. Generality of Capital', Marx presents the process of reproduction of capital as apparently eternal, but then he reveals the way that accumulation is dependent on given historical conditions. At the beginning of his 'Chapter on Capital' in the *Grundrisse*, he assumes that the basic conditions of capitalism are presupposed, and he traces them logically as reproduction takes place through capital accumulation. This necessitates another discussion of the way that these 'primitive' conditions are posited historically. In other words his theory of primitive accumulation[8] requires a theory of the accumulation of capital, which he uses as a criterion for discovering what kinds of conditions gave rise to capitalism in the past.

Marx's study of primitive accumulation is limited to an account of the way that surplus-value is generated as primitive accumulation takes place. The predominant forms of capital were mercantile capital and usury. Both forms were often linked as the surplus-labour of independent small-scale producers was absorbed as mercantile profit or interest through the putting-out system. In that way independent producers were transformed into wage-labourers as their independence became merely nominal. Eventually they were organised into manufacture, which was then transformed into industrial capital.

The commodity-relation gains ground, and the degree of this transformation — 'primitive accumulation' — can be measured. When the commodity-relation covers not only a surplus-product but also the necessary product — the fund to reproduce the labour-power of the producer — labour-power itself becomes a commodity. When the necessary product has become a commodity, labour-power is alienated from the products necessary for its own reproduction, because they are the property of another person, i.e. the capitalist. Workers buy necessary products with the money which they earn as wages. In short, there are four instances of transformation: mercantile capital into industrial capital; surplus-value from mercantile profit into industrial profit; necessary products into commodities; and labour-power into a commodity.[9]

Marx quotes Smith's descriptions of commercial capital in *The wealth of nations* from notes that he made on the French edition, just before writing the *Economic and philosophical manuscripts (1844)*. Marx aims to show that capitalism is never a closed, eternal system, but one with an origin in the past.

Then with his theory of 'disposable time' Marx puts the future of capitalism into perspective. He has already demonstrated why, in his view, capitalism will cease to exist. He has done this through his analysis in 'II. Particularity of Capital' of the way that machinery or fixed capital develops. Here again he points out that capitalism will vanish in future, losing its presuppositions. These are the presuppositions on which the alienated relation between the capitalist and the wage-labourer is grounded:

> . . . this twisting and inversion [i.e. the conversion of actualization of labour into the loss of actuality] is a *real* [*phenomenon*], not a *merely supposed one* existing merely in the imagination of the labourers and the capitalists. But obviously this process of inversion is a merely *historical* necessity [*bloss*

> *historische Notwendigkeit*], a necessity for the development of the productive forces solely from a specific point of departure [i.e. primitive accumulation], or basis, but in no way an *absolute* necessity [*eine absolute Notwendigkeit*] of production; rather, a vanishing one, and the result and the purpose (immanent) of this process is to transcend this basis itself, together with this form of the process. The bourgeois economists are so much cooped up within the representations of a determinate historic stage of development of society that the necessity of the *objectification* [*die Notwendigkeit der Vergegenständlichung*] of the social powers of labour appears to them as inseparable from the necessity of their *alienation* [*die Notwendigkeit der Entfremdung*] *vis-à-vis* living labour (N 831–2, M 698; quotation partially altered).

Evidently Marx intends to critise not only the bourgeois political economists, but also Hegel, since he comments that the alienation of wage-labourers is never 'an *absolute* necessity', but 'a merely *historical* necessity'. Therefore it is not 'a supposed' phenomenon 'existing merely in the imagination of the labourers and the capitalists', but 'a *real* [phenomenon]'.

For Marx, Hegel's idealism is not merely philosophical speculation. It is rather a real expression of the relations of modern private property. It is a philosophical expression of its own economic background, i.e. the relation of value and capital. As the basic relation of modern bourgeois society, it is inevitably conditioned by real persons when it actually appears. For that reason Marx critically suggests that Hegel's *Logic*, in which an ideal subject or 'idea' appears to posit itself and all other objects, is similar to political economy, in which value and capital do likewise.

Marx foresees the transcendence of capitalist alienation and the possibility of the realisation of freedom:

> But with the transcendence of the *immediate* character of living labour, as merely *individual*, or as general merely internally [i.e. spiritually] or merely externally [i.e. physically],[10] with the positing of the activity of individuals as immediately general or *social* activity, the objective moments of production are stripped of this form of alienation; they are thereby posited as property, as the organic social body [*der organische gesellschaftliche Leib*] within which the individuals reproduce them-

selves as individuals, but as social individuals (N 832, M 698; quotation partially altered).

We have already seen that Aristotle's theory of cause is applied by Marx in his demonstration of the way the alienation of the wage-labourer will be transcended as capitalist society develops. Here in 'III. Individuality of Capital' he also relates this to 'disposable time'. In the production of relative surplus-value, he writes:

> . . . the possibility of which [i.e. greater productive force of labour] is already posited in the presupposed growth of the population and [its] training to labour (with which determinate free time [*bestimmte freie Zeit*] is also posited for the non-labouring, not directly labouring population, hence development of spiritual capacities etc.; spiritual [*geistig*] appropriation of nature) (N 774, M 645; quotation largely altered).

Potential free time in capitalist society appears in alienated forms and is only partially appropriated by the non-labouring population. However, workers gradually become aware that potential free time is an estranged form of their own productive force, and that it is stimulated as productive forces develop their collective and scientific labour. This process, in which the consciousness of workers develops, is also the process in which their forces are regained. Free 'disposable time' will be realised for them as true wealth. Marx's perspective is based on his recognition of capitalist alienation and propertylessness as a 'merely *historical* necessity'. He grasps the history of alienation as a phenomenological process, so freedom becomes possible when capitalist alienation is recognised as a historical necessity. That historical necessity, in Marx's view, will eventually vanish, and he supports that judgement with his critique of political economy.

By contrast Hegel asserts that freedom consists in knowing 'absolute necessity' and nothing more:

> . . . the process of necessity is so directed that it overcomes the rigid externality which it first had and reveals its inwardness, by which it then presents what are bound together as not factually alien to each other, but other moments of *a* whole [*ein Ganze*], each of which, in its relation to the other, is with

itself and combines with itself. This is the transfiguration of necessity into freedom (sect. 158, Z; quotation largely altered).

'The process of necessity' mentioned above appears at first glance to be very similar to the way Marx sees capital. He starts from money-capital as 'a whole' and in the end reveals it be 'one determinate totality' in which various moments are bound up with each other. And he shares with Hegel an understanding that knowledge involves tracing a process of necessity.

However, Hegel stays within the sphere of cognition, because for him 'knowing' (*wissen*) is practice itself. He thinks that the world or cosmos is created in such a way that 'knowing' objectifies itself, and that 'knowing' comes to know itself. For him the universe is what 'knowing' knows. What is objectified is nothing but 'knowing' itself, so for him knowledge alone can count as practice. 'Knowing' is thus the substance of all that is objectified (i.e. that which has the appearance of an object) and presents itself as subject through its spiritual labour of objectification. Necessity for Hegel implies this process of 'knowing' coming to know itself. When 'knowing' comes to know itself thoroughly, it is transfigured into freedom, which is, in other words, 'absolute knowing' (*absolute Wissen*). For Hegel necessity does not vanish but reappears as freedom.

For Marx, necessity as an object of historical knowledge is a historical necessity, e.g. capital. In the process of tracing capital from 'a whole' to 'one determinate totality', he reveals the real possibility of practical transcendence. Exposing the genesis of capital indicates to wage-labourers a possibility for emancipation. Wage-labourers will develop step by step a consciousness alternative to the bourgeois value-consciousness prevalent in capitalist society. In that way they come to recognise that the force of capital is in fact a perverse form of their own potential. Marx's task is to grasp capitalism as a historical necessity, vanishing in future, and to show that it is accompanied by the discovery of the real human subject in practice and the possibility for realising freedom for all.

Freedom for Hegel is limited to the *theoria* of 'absolute necessity'. For Marx, theoretical recognition of the possibility for freedom embodies a specific claim. His claim is that the possibility for freedom can be changed into an actuality, and that such a criterion of realisation is an appropriate one against which to test his theory.[11] Thus he points out the mission (*Aufgabe*) to realise this possibility for human freedom that rests with the working class. In his critique of political economy he characterises contemporary capitalism as the last system of private property, or the last stage of prehistory (*Vorgeschichte*) of class societies in the natural history of mankind. The subjective and objective conditions for advancing to human history proper, a classless society, thus mature in capitalism:

> . . . it is evident that the material productive force already present, already worked out, existing in the form of fixed capital, together with the scientific power and the population etc., in short all conditions of wealth, that the greatest conditions for the reproduction of wealth, i.e. the abundant development of the social individual — that the development of the productive forces brought about by the historical development of capital itself, when it reaches a certain point, transcends the self-increasing value [*Selbstverwertung*] of capital, instead of positing it. Beyond a certain point, the development of the productive forces becomes a barrier [*Schranke*] for capital; hence the capital relation [becomes] a barrier for the development of the productive forces of labour. When it has reached this point, capital, i.e. wage-labour, enters into the same relation, [tending] towards the development of social wealth and productive forces, as the guild system, serfdom, slavery [*Zunftwesen, Leibeigenschaft, Sklaverei*], and is necessarily stripped off as a fetter. The last shape of servitude [*die letzte Knechtsgestalt*], which human activity assumes, that of wage-labour, on one side, capital on the other, is thereby cast off like a skin, and this casting-off itself is the result of the mode of production corresponding to capital; material and mental conditions of the negation of wage-labour and of capital, themselves already the negation of earlier forms of unfree social production, are themselves results of its production process (N 749, M 622–3).

In the passage above from the *Grundrisse* Marx comes to a conclusion that enables him to rewrite his manuscript 'Chapter on Money'. That rewritten version is the so-called original text of *A contribution to the critique of political economy*, and after completing that draft, he prepared the finished manuscript for publication. In the famous Preface[12] to that work, published in 1859, he describes capitalism as the last stage of the prehistory of mankind, a point of entry into its universal history.

Appendix

Theoretical Analysis of the *Grundrisse*

This analysis breaks the major chapters of the *Grundrisse* into sections that relate topically to Marx's later work in *Capital*.

The 'Chapter on Money'

1. Critique of Alfred Darimon (N 115–40, M 49–75)
2. Transformation of product into commodity (N 140–3, M 75–7)
3. Transformation of commodity into money (N 143–56, M 77–89)
4. Economic interdependence in history (N 156–71, M 89–102)
5. Economy of time (N 171–3, M 102–4)
6. Circulation of commodities — 1 (N 173–203, M 104–32)
7. Value-form and process of exchange (N 203–8, M 132–6)
8. Circulation of commodities — 2 (N 208–15, M 136–42)
9. Transition of money to capital — 1 (N 215–50, M 142–73); see Chapter 3, note 1 below.

The 'Chapter on Capital'

'I. Generality of Capital'

1. Transition of money to capital — 2 (N 250–66, M 173–88)
2. Exchange between capital and labour (N 266–97, M 188–217)
3. Labour-process (N 297–310, M 218–29)
4. Valorisation process (N 310–26, M 229–42)
5. Previous theories of surplus-value — 1 (N 326–33, M 242–8)
6. Relative surplus-value (N 333–53, M 248–66)
7. Twofold character of labour (N 354–66, M 266–77)
8. Results of the process of production — 1 (N 366–401, M 277–309)
9. Process of realisation of capital — 1 (N 401–23, M 315–36)
10. Results of the process of production — 2 (N 423–34, M 336–45)

11. Process of realisation of capital — 2 (N 434, M 345)
12. Formation of the general rate of profit (N 434–9, M 345–50)
13. Process of reproduction through exchange (N 439–47, M 350–7)
14. Process of realisation of capital — 3 (N 447–50, M 357–9)
15. Surplus product and surplus-capital (N 450–6, M 360–5)
16. Conversion of the law of appropriation (N 456–8, M 365–7)
17. Reproduction of the capital-relation (N 458, M 367)
18. Pre-capitalist economic formations (N 459–515, M 367–417); see Chapter 3, note 3 below.

'II. Particularity of Capital'

1. Circuit of capital (N 516–49, M 417–46)
2. Previous theories of surplus-value — 2 (N 549–618, M 446–505)
3. Turnover of capital (N 618–721, M 505–97)
4. Reproduction of one capital through simple circulation (N 721–43, M 597–616)

'III. Individuality of Capital'

1. Capital and profit (N 745–6, M 619–20)
2. Decline in the general rate of profit — 1 (N 746–58, M 620–30)
3. Form of production and form of distribution (N 758–9, M 630–2)
4. Cost of production (N 759–61, M 632–3)
5. Decline in the general rate of profit — 2 (N 761–4, M 633–6)
6. Co-operation, division of labour, and machinery (N 765–78, M 636–47)
7. Previous theories of money — 1 (N 778–818, M 648–83)
8. Machinery (N 818–31, M 683–97)
9. Alienation of labour (N 831–3, M 697–9)
10. Previous theories of money — 2 (N 833–51, M 699–714)
11. Profit, interest and merchants' wealth (N 851–61, M 714–23)
12. Previous theories of money — 3 (N 861–78, M 724–38)
13. Capital and interest (N 878–80, M 738–9)

Notes

Details of publication, where not otherwise indicated, can be found in the Select Bibliography.

Preface

1. For bibliographical details of my Japanese writings, which I have translated into English myself and included in the present volume, see Acknowledgements and the entries under Uchida, H., in the Select Bibliography.

2. There are two texts of Hegel's *Logic*: the so-called 'Major Logic' (*Science of logic*) and the 'Minor Logic' (a section from the *Encyclopaedia of the philosophical sciences*). The *Logic* which Marx read whilst writing the *Grundrisse* is assumed to have been the 'Major Logic'. Quotations in this book, however, are mainly from the 'Minor Logic', for ease of interpretation. References to the 'Major Logic', as well as to the 'Minor Logic', are appended to each citation.

3. *Werke*, vol. 29, p. 260.

4. Rosdolsky, *The making of Marx's Capital*, p. xi.

5. Rosdolsky, p. xi.

6. Rosdolsky, p. xiii.

7. *Werke*, vol. 30, p. 207.

8. In the 'Chapter on Money': 'negation of the negation' (p. 103), 'mediation' (p. 112), 'becoming' (p. 114), 'logical contradiction' (p. 119), 'intermediary' (p. 127), 'contradiction' (between use-value and exchange-value) (p. 133), 'simple infinite process' (p. 142). In the 'Chapter on Capital': 'remaining at home with itself' (*Beisichbleiben*) (p. 187), 'boundary' (*Grenze*) and 'barrier' (*Schranke*) (p. 188), 'for itself' (p. 210), 'ruse' (*List*) (p. 228), 'living contradiction' (p. 249), 'realization' or 'actualization' (*Verwirklichung*) and 'de-realization' or 'loss of actuality' (*Entwirklichung*) (p. 259), 'recall' (p. 325), 'indifference' (p. 332), 'the essence must appear' (p. 368).

9. N 32. See also David McLellan's 'Comment on Jean-Yves Calvez *Hegel and Marx*', in O'Malley *et al.* (eds), *The legacy of Hegel*, p. 107: 'In this unique writing [*Grundrisse*] Marx's debt to Hegel and his method, with emphasis on the *Logic* rather than on the *Phenomenology*, comes through quite as strikingly as in the *Paris Manuscripts*. There are an enormous number of Hegelian elements in it.'

10. Martin Nicolaus remarks that in the *Logic* 'identity' and 'mediation' are unconditional and absolute (cf. N 41). This relates to Hegel's 'form' which subsumes 'substance', 'matter' and 'content' under itself, (see Chapter 3, section 2 of the present work). However, Hegel unconsciously presents the logical process as the absolute mediator or

abstract thinker, who is privileged to exist both within the process and outside it.

11. In the 'Chapter on Money': 'abstract identity' (N 137), 'bad infinity' (N 197), 'being-for-itself' and 'being-for-another' (N 244). In the 'Chapter on Capital': 'returning into ground' (N 255), 'becoming and finitude' (N 260), 'mechanism' (N 301, 312), 'judgement' (N 310), 'boundary and barrier' (N 334), 'form and matter' (N 360), 'relative necessity' (N 401), 'being-for-itself' in 'measure' (N 448), 'universality' or 'generality' (*Allgemeinheit*), 'particularity' and 'individuality' (N 450), 'process which alters form without positing new content' (N 536), 'teleology' (N 734).

12. N 255, M 177.

13. N 233, M 157.

14. N 302, M 221. The same mistranslation is found in a recent English translation by Ernst Wangermann of the first half of the *Grundrisse* under the title 'Economic manuscripts of 1857–58 (First Version of *Capital*)' in Karl Marx and Frederick Engels, *Collected Works*, vol. 28 (London: Lawrence & Wishart, 1986), p. 228. Wangermann ignores most of Nicolaus's footnotes that refer to Hegel's *Logic*. For example, though Nicolaus does not recognise the connection between 'ground' and 'a contradiction which dissolves itself', he footnotes the term 'ground' to Hegel's *Logic*, a link that Wangermann ignores. Wangermann notes only one connection between the *Science of logic* and the *Grundrisse*, probably following *Marx-Engels Gesamtausgabe (MEGA)*, II/1. Cf. 'Index of Quoted and Mentioned Literature', Marx and Engels, *Collected works*, vol. 28, p. 570.

15. Readers should also consult McTaggart, *A commentary on Hegel's Logic*, or Mure, *A study of Hegel's Logic*. The difficulties in translating Hegel's terminology are discussed, for example, by Martin Milligan in his 'Translator's Note' to Karl Marx, *Economic–philosophic manuscripts* (New York: International Publishers, 1964), and by Arthur in a note to his *Dialectics of labour*.

16. Schmidt, *The concept of nature in Marx*, p. 213.

17. *Werke*, vol. 29, p. 547. The Japanese philosopher Kitaro Nishida has studied the Marx–Aristotle relationship. Writing before World War II, he used the old *MEGA*, published in the 1920s and 1930s. Nishida argues that Marx attached more importance to Aristotle than to Hegel, but the relationship has not been much noticed elsewhere.

18. Martin Nicolaus remarks: 'The question of the proper beginning remains unsettled in Marx's Introduction . . . To find the proper beginning . . . one must turn to the very last page of the *Grundrisse*'s seventh notebook [N 881], a section Marx subtitled "1) Value [*Wert*]" ' (N 37). However, this comment is insufficient. Firstly, it is by virtue of grasping the twofold character of labour that Marx could define the product of capital as the commodity (C + V + S). The most abstract determination of this is the simple commodity, which is the appropriate starting point. He thus abandoned the idea of beginning with 'production in general'. Secondly, Nicolaus overlooks the fact that Marx began with 'the concrete, the determinate, and hence . . . the contradictory in itself' (N 38) in the 'Chapter on Money'. 'Product in exchange', which Marx

put at the beginning of the 'Chapter on Money', is what Nicolaus claims is 'a materialist beginning' (N 38), referring to Aristotle's categories of primary and secondary substance.

19. Schmidt, *Concept of nature in Marx*, p. 234.

20. Cf. 'Eine Übersetzung Hegels zu *De Anima* III, 4–5, mitgeteilt und erläutert von Walter Kern', *Hegel Studien*, vol. 1 (1961), pp. 49–88.

21. Cf. Uchida, 'The money of the spirit'. C. J. Arthur has clarified the relationship between Marx and Hegel (and between Marx and French socialism) in the *Economic and philosophical manuscripts (1844)* with respect to Hegel's *Phenomenology*, but he has not recognised other important uses of the 'Minor Logic' in the manuscripts. He merely notes various aspects of Hegel's *Logic* as Marx uses them in the formation of *Capital*, cf. *Dialectics of labour*, p. 125: Marx uses Hegel's *Logic* in getting 'his economics into shape', but for Arthur this is 'too cryptic to construe easily'.

22. Cf. The Introduction to O'Malley and Schrader, 'Marx's précis of Hegel's doctrine of being in the *Minor Logic*', pp. 423–31.

23. *Capital*, vol. 1, pp. 102–3.

24. Carver, 'Marx — and Hegel's *Logic*'. See also his *Marx's social theory*, p. 47.

25. *Werke*, vol. 31, p. 133. Cf. 'a relative whole' in Marx's letter of 11 March 1858 to Ferdinand Lassalle (*Werke*, vol. 29, p. 554), or 'a whole' in his letter of 2 October 1859 to Lassalle (*Werke*, vol. 29, p. 613).

26. *Manuscripts (1844)*, p. 383.

27. Cf. Takeyoshi Kawashima, *The theory of property law* (*Shoyukenho no Riron*) (Tokyo: Iwanami Shoten, 1949).

Chapter I

1. Cf. *Science of logic*, pp. 764–72.

2. Cf. *Science of logic*, pp. 767 ff.

3. Cf. *Science of logic*, pp. 772–4.

4. Cf. 'In copulation the immediacy of the living individuality perishes; the death of this life is the procession of spirit' (*Science of logic*, p. 774). See note 20 in the Preface of the present work; see also Spicer, *Aristotle's conception of the soul*, pp. 103–17, 130–4.

5. Cf. Yoshiki Yoshizawa, 'The consummation of the classical political economy — 1817 and David Ricardo', in Yuzo Deguchi (ed.), *The history of economic theories (Keizaigakushi)*, (Kyoto: Minerva, 1952). In his article Professor Yoshizawa defines Ricardo's theory of distribution as the consummation of the classical theory of accumulation, using the second section of Marx's Introduction to the *Grundrisse*.

6. Cf. *Science of logic*, p. 786 ff.

7. Cf. *Science of logic*, p. 793 ff.

8. Cf. The two plans in the 'Chapter on Capital' (N 264, M 187; N 275–6, M 199–200). In the process in which 'capital in general' in the *Grundrisse* subsumes 'generality, particularity and individuality' under itself through negation, Marx follows this definition of 'generality' from Hegel: 'As negativity in general or in accordance with the *first*, *immediate*

negation, the general [*das Allgemeine*] contains determinateness generally as *particularity*; as the *second* negation, that is, as negation of the negation, it is *absolute determinateness* or *individuality* and *concreteness*' (*Science of logic*, p. 603; quotation partially altered).

9. It is noteworthy that Marx rarely uses the term 'capitalism' (*Kapitalismus*). It does not appear at all in the *Grundrisse*, only a few times in the *Critique of political economy 1861–3*, e.g. *Marx–Engels Werke*, vol. 26.2, p. 493, and but once in *Capital*, vol. 2, p. 199. The term is used merely for convenience in the present work.

10. *Science of logic*, pp. 801–2; quotation partially altered.

11. Cf. O'Malley, 'Marx's "economics" and Hegel's *Philosophy of right*'. In this article O'Malley analyses the relation between the plan in the Introduction to the *Grundrisse* and Hegel's *Philosophy of right* and *Encyclopaedia*.

12. Cf. *Science of logic*, pp. 803 ff., where *Einteilung* is translated as 'division'.

13. N 450, M 359.

14. Cf. Hiroshi Uchida, 'A study of the Introduction to the *Grundrisse*' ('Keizaigakuhihanyoko Jyosetsu no Kenkyu'), in *Annual Bulletin of the Institute for Social Sciences of Senshu University* (Tokyo), 1977.

15. Hans-Jürgen Krahl writes that metaphysical consciousness, which oppresses our individuality, is capital or exchange-value, which are merely abstractions, and that Hegel defines capital metaphysically. He also suggests that Hegel's *Logic* indicates the intersubjectivity and forms of intercourse which represented emancipation in the bourgeois revolution ('Bemerkungen zum Verhältnis von Kapital und Hegelscher Wesenlogik', pp. 145, 147).

Following Krahl, Walter Neumann asserts that the determinations of society are economic *par excellence*, as Marx analysed them, and that this is true for Hegel, too, even though he was not conscious of this and did not think that he was using 'production' as a paradigm. Cf. *Der unbewusste Hegel*, p. 11. Neumann argues that the simple commodity in *Capital* corresponds to the 'doctrine of being' in Hegel's *Logic*, from which arises 'commodity consciousness' (*Warenbewusstsein*), which he defines as 'the spirit of man as private proprietor, the spirit or the character of commodity' (p. 23).

Thomas T. Sekine, translator of Kozo Uno, *Principles of political economy: theory of a purely capitalist society* (Brighton: Harvester Press, 1980), tries to clarify the correspondence of *Capital* to Hegel's *Logic*, rearranging *Capital* according to Uno's theory. But Sekine does not explain why his rearranged *Capital* corresponds to the *Logic* any more directly than *Capital* itself; cf. *Dialectic of capital*.

Chapter 2

1. Cf. Hegel's *Logic*, sect. 115 ('Identity'), sect. 116 ('Difference'), sect. 119 ('Opposition'), sect. 120 ('Contradiction'); Hegel, *Science of logic*, pp. 411 ff. ('Identity'), pp. 417 ff. ('Difference'), pp. 424 ff. ('Opposition'), pp. 431 ff. ('Contradiction').

2. Cf. *Science of logic*, pp. 419 ff.

3. Cf. 'They [likeness and unlikeness] have, namely the [merely] *implicit* reflection outside them, or are the likeness and unlikeness of *a third party* [*ein Drittes*], of an other than they' (*Science of logic*, p. 421).

4.Cf. *Science of logic*, pp. 157 ff.

5. In a note to the *German ideology*, Marx writes: '*Relation for the Philosophers = idea.* They know only the relation "*of* man" to himself, and therefore all real relations become ideas for them to them'; *Die deutsche Ideologie*, ed. W. Hiromatsu (German text and Japanese *apparatus criticus*) (Tokyo: Kawadeshoboshinsha, 1974), p. 150; my English translation — HU; cf. Chapter 5, note 8 below.

In the *Critique of political economy, 1861–3*, the second version of the draft for *Capital*, Marx writes: '*Value* is based on the fact that men relate to their labours as equal and general labour and as social labour in this form. This is an abstraction like all human thought, and social relations exist only among men, so far as they think and possess this ability to abstract from sensuous individuality and accidentality' (*Marx-Engels Gesamtausgabe (MEGA)*, II/3.1, p. 210.

6. Cf. 'as a purely objective form, [as] individuals external and accidental to form of wealth [*als einer rein dinglichen Form, den Individuen gegenüber äusserlichen und zufälligen Form des Reichtums*]' (N 235, M 158).

7. Aristotle, *Metaphysics* 1017b 23–6; cf. *The complete works of Aristotle*, p. 1607.

8. *Aristotles' Metaphysik*, vol. 2, Book VII(Z)–XIV(N), trans. Hermann Bonitz (Hamburg: Felix Meiner Verlag, 1980), p. 81.

9. *Aristotles' Metaphysik*, ed. and trans. Franz F. Schwarz (Ditzingen, West Germany: Reclam, 1970), p. 208.

10. *Capital*, vol. 1, p. 126.

11. Cf. *Capital*, vol. 1, p. 198.

12. Cf. Smith, *The wealth of nations*, vol. 1, p. 25.

13. *Phenomenology of spirit*, p. 481; quotation partially altered.

14. *Phenomenology of spirit*, p. 482.

15. Cf. 'the language of commodities' (*Capital*, vol. 1, p. 143).

16. The term 'abstraction' derives from Marx's work in the *Economic and philosophical manuscripts (1844)* and continues in use in the *Grundrisse*, along with other terms, including 'alienation', 'thinghood' (in conjunction with 'reification'), 'substance as subject', 'attribute of money', 'power of money', 'vanishing' and 'selfish man' (in conjunction with 'value').

17. *Capital*, vol. 1, p. 144.

18. *Manuscripts (1844)*, p. 382.

19. *Manuscripts (1844)*, p. 388.

20. *Manuscripts (1844)*, p. 386; quotation partially altered.

21. *Manuscripts (1844)*, p. 392.

22. *Manuscripts (1844)*, p. 387.

23. *Manuscripts (1844)*, p. 388; quotation partially altered.

24. *Manuscripts (1844)*, p. 389.

25. *Manuscripts (1844)*, p. 379.

26. With reference to Hegel's 'magnitude' (*Grösse*) (*Logic*, sects. 99–100) in the 'Doctrine of being', Marx writes: 'While a product (or

activity) becomes exchange-value, it is not only transformed into a definite quantitative relation, a relation number [*ein Verhältniszahl*] . . . but it must also at the same time be transformed qualitatively, be transposed into another element, so that both commodities become named magnitides [*benannte Grössen*], of the same unit, i.e. commensurable' (N 143, M 78; quotation largely altered).

27. Cf. *Science of logic*, pp. 202 ff; '*Amount* and *unit* constitute the *moments* of number'; *Science of logic*, p. 203.

28. 'What is clear from the *Grundrisse*'s discussion of value . . . is that Marx is discussing categories in the context of their process of coming-to-be' (Meikle, *Essentialism in the thought of Karl Marx*, p. 146). Those who reject the view that Marx's use of Hegel in the *Grundrisse* is significant invariably quote the following comment by Marx: 'It will be necessary later, before this question is dropped, to correct the idealist manner of the presentation, which makes it seem as if it were merely a matter of conceptual determinations and of the dialectic of these concepts. Above all in the case of the phrase: product (or activity) becomes commodity; commodity, exchange-value; exchange-value, money' (N 151, M 85). However, this comment does not mean that Marx abandoned his use of Hegel, but rather indicates the necessity of replacing 'the commodity becomes money' with 'value-form and the process of exchange', where Marx applies Hegel's logic of 'one and many'!

29. Cf. '. . . the image of true infinity, bent back into itself, becomes the *circle* [*Kreis*], the line which has reached itself, which is closed and wholly present, without *beginning* and *end*' (*Science of logic*, p. 149).

Marx's comparison of the 'labour process', the end of which consists in the consumption of the product of labour, with 'the circulation of value', the end of which consists in circulation itself or 'value-in-process', is based on a distinction between *poiēsis* and *praxis* made by Aristotle: '. . . while making [*poiēsis*] has an end other than itself, action [*praxis*] cannot; for good action itself is its end' (*Nicomachean ethics* 1140b 6–7, *The complete works of Aristotle*, vol. 2, p. 1800). However, Marx thinks that action (*praxis*) which mediates the circulation of value is merely alienated praxis.

30. Cf. '. . . it [infinity] therefore essentially contains its other and is, consequently, in its own self the other of itself' (*Science of logic*, p. 146).

31. In one of Marx's commentaries on the political economists he writes that commodity-exchange originates from surplus products exchanged between communities, and that as soon as the conversion of the product into a commodity spreads to necessary products, the factors of capitalist production are beginning to arise (Marx, 'Excerpts from James Mill's *Elements of political economy*', trans. Rodney Livingstone, in *Early writings*, pp. 269–70).

32. Cf. *Science of logic*, pp. 170 ff.

33. Cf. 'I [*Ich*] is for I, both are the same, the I is twice named, but so that each of the two is only a "for-one", is ideal; spirit is only for spirit . . . Self-consciousness, however, as consciousness, enters into the difference *of itself* and an *other* — or of its *ideality*, in which it produces conceptions, and of its *reality*, inasmuch as its conception has a determinate content which has the side of being known as the unsublated negative, as a real, determinate being' (*Science of logic*, p. 160; quotation partially altered).

34. Hegel, *First philosophy of spirit*, p. 249; quotation partially altered. Exactly when Hegel became acquainted with Smith's *The wealth of nations* is a matter of debate. Georg Lukács writes: 'It is . . . almost certain that Hegel was acquainted with Adam Smith right from the beginning of his period in Jena [1801 – 6 — HU]', *The young Hegel*, p. 172. However, H. S. Harris is more precise: 'It [Smith's *The wealth of nations*] was translated by Garve and published in German between 1796 and 1799. Hegel first refers to it explicitly in his first 'Philosophy of spirit' of 1804. The edition from which he quotes there was apparently the Basel edition of 1791 (in English). He owned this edition, but we do not know when he acquired it; obviously, however, he would be more likely to purchase it *while* he was in Switzerland [i.e. his period in Berne 1793 – 6 — HU], and *before* the German translation was available' (Hegel, *First philosophy of spirit*, p. 95; see Chapter 3, note 28 below).

35. In *The wealth of nations* Smith presupposes three propensities which underlie civilised society: to exchange (Book I, Chapter 2), to be industrious in work (Book I, Chapter 8), and to save and invest (Book II, Chapters 3, 5).

36. *Manuscripts (1844)*, p. 389. Marx adopts Aristotle's view of natural history from 'De anima', when he writes: 'We also see that only naturalism is capable of comprehending the process of world history' (*Manuscripts (1844)*, p. 389).

37. Cf. 'Such a particular [*Einzelne*] which contains within itself all really present species [*Arten*] of the same entity is one *general* [*ein Allgemeine*]'; from 'The Commodity', Chapter 1 of the first edition (1867) of *Capital*, vol. 1, in *Value — Studies by Marx*, p. 27; *Marx-Engels Gesamtausgabe (MEGA)*, II/5, p. 37.

38. *Marx-Engels Gesamtausgabe (MEGA)*, II/2, p. 117.

39. 'Value-form' and 'process of exchange' are later separated by Marx in the first edition (1867) of *Capital*, vol. 1, after he had completed his *Critique of political economy 1861 – 3*. There he changed his plan for 'capital in general' or 'one capital', introducing new moments of competition between 'many capitals' and their interdependency in the reproduction-process. At the most abstract level in theory, this causes 'process of exchange' and 'value-form' to separate. 'Process of exchange' is the simplest determination in the reproduction of value and use-value through circulation, whereas 'value-form' is the simplest reflection in the immediate accumulation of value.

40. Cf. N 801 ff., M 668 ff.

41. Cf. 'We saw that money can be piled up in part [*zum Teil*] by way of the sheer exchange of equivalents; but this forms so insignificant a source [*eine so unbedeutende Quelles*] that it is not worth mentioning historically — if it is presupposed that this money is gained through the exchange of one's own labour' (N 504, M 407).

'The formation of capital does not emerge from landed property (here at most from the *tenant* [*Pächter*] in so far as he is a dealer in agricultural products); nor from the guild (although there is a possibility at the last point); but rather from merchant's and usurer's wealth [*Kaufmanns- und Wuchervermögen*]' (N 505, M 407).

42. Cf. *Capital*, vol. 3, pp. 452 f.

43. Between the *Grundrisse* of 1857–8 and the principal manuscripts for *Capital*, vol. 3 (written between 1864 and 1865), Marx drastically changes his opinion concerning the historical genesis of capitalism. In the *Grundrisse* Marx writes: . . . capital arises only where trade has seized possession of production itself, and where the merchant becomes producer, or the producer mere merchant . . . But the rise of capital in its adequate form presupposes it as commercial capital' (N 859, M 721). However, in the manuscripts for *Capital*, vol 3, he writes the opposite: 'The producer may become a merchant and capitalist . . . this is the really revolutionary way. Alternatively, however, the merchant may take direct control of production himself . . . it cannot bring about the overthrow of the old mode of production by itself, but rather preserves and retains it as its own precondition' (*Capital*, vol. 3, p. 452).

This change derives from his recognition in *A contribution to the critique of political economy* of 1859 and the *Critique of political economy of 1861–3*, that the formula for the circuit of commodity-capital (C' . . . C') as the unity of the production and circulation of capital is the basic paradigm to use in grasping capital, and that the most abstract category for this is the simple commodity, the unity of the determinations of production and circulation. This view is first expressed in published form at the opening of *A contribution to the critique of political economy* of 1859, and it follows from his description of the commodity under '1) Value' in his seventh notebook of the *Grundrisse* manuscripts. The economic subjects who unite production and circulation were independent small-scale producers of the simple commodity, who were to be divided between two opposite poles, capitalist and wage-labourer. This division is Marx's 'really revolutionary way' of grasping the historical genesis of capitalism.

It is noteworthy that in Chapter 20 of *Capital*, vol. 3, Marx cites the same material from Smith's *The wealth of nations* that he does in the *Grundrisse* (N 857–8; *Capital*, vol. 3, pp. 443–52).

In his *Spirit of capitalism* Professor Hisao Otsuka insists that in a 'local market area' the law of value brings about economic inequality amongst independent small-scale producers who, he presumes, form the basis of the capital-relation. However, his application of the law of value to an alleged 'local market area' is inconsistent with Marx's procedure in the *Grundrisse* and in the first (1867) and second (1872) German editions of *Capital*, since Marx argues that the law of value begins to operate just when the capital-relation is realised, so in his view the following transformations coincide: the commodity into money, money into capital, and the labour-force into a commodity.

44. Cf. *Science of logic*, p. 371 ff.

45. Cf. *Science of logic*, pp. 383 ff.

46. *Science of logic*, p. 442; quotation partially altered.

Chapter 3

1. In my article 'An editorial problem of the *Grundrisse*' ('Keizaigakuhihanyoko no Henshumondai'), in *The Grundrisse commentaries*

(*Commentaries Keizaigakuhihanyoko*), II (Tokyo: Nihonhyoronsha, 1974), I have pointed out that the editors of the *Grundrisse* (East Berlin: Dietz Verlag, 1953), were incorrect in judging that the 'Chapter on Money' ends at the conclusion of Notebook II, p. 7, and that the 'Chapter on Capital' begins at the top of p. 8 in the same notebook. The editors of the *Ökonomische Manuskripte 1857/58*, repeated the error. Though Marx wrote the title 'Chapter on Money as Capital' at the head of p. 8, he did not then discuss anything that relates to the title but wrote about 'money as money' up to the middle of p. 12 (*Marx–Engels Gesamtausgabe (MEGA)* II/1.1, p. 173, l. 30). After that he began to write about 'money as capital'. Evidence for my view is as follows:

a. Marx's letters to Engels of 2 April 1858, in which Marx revealed that his plan for the 'Chapter on Money' ends in (d) [the law of appropriation including a critique of F. Bastiat, H. C. Carey and the Proudhonists]. This corresponds to his material between p. 7 and the middle of p. 12 of Notebook II (*Marx–Engels Gesamtausgabe (MEGA)*, II/1.1, pp. 160–73).

b. Marx's Index to his seven notebooks, which shows that he intended to discuss, as the last but one item of the 'Chapter on Money', (5) the law of appropriation, which appears in simple circulation (*Marx–Engels Gesamtausgabe (MEGA)*, II/2, p. 7.

c. In Marx'a *Urtext of the critique of political economy*, under (5) the phenomenon of the law of appropriation in simple circulation, we find many of the same sentences as are found between pp. 7 and 12 of Notebook II, and no material from subsequent passages in the 'Chapter on Capital'.

d. Marx's 'References (*Referate*) to my own Notebooks', in which he writes '*Notebook II*. Simple Exchange. *Relations of Exchangers*. Equality. Freedom etc. Harmonies. (7–9, 10). (Bastiat. Proudhon.) (11–12)/ Capital. *The Amount of Value*. (12) Landed property and Capital. (13) Capital originates from circulation. Exchange-value [is] content' (*Marx–Engels Gesamtausgabe (MEGA)*, II/2, p. 275).

e. Marx's letter of 1 February 1859 to Joseph Weydemeyer, in which he explained: 'In these two chapters [the chapter on the commodity and the chapter on money or simple circulation], the Proudhonist socialism now fashionable in France, which wants to retain private production, *but organizes* the exchange of private products, i.e. which wants *commodity*, but does not need *money*, is, at the same time, to be completely destroyed. Communism has, first of all, to dispose of the "false brother"' (*Werke*, vol. 29, p. 573).

This evidence indicates that the revised edition of the *Grundrisse* should be published with the manuscripts from the top of p. 8 to the middle of p. 12 of Notebook II appearing in the 'Chapter on Money', not in the 'Chapter on Capital'.

2. The transformation of the product into a commodity is related to the transformation of labour-power into a commodity. When most products, which make up the means of production and consumption, have become commodities, labour-power is reproduced through the purchase and consumption of the means of life, which are commodities under the control of capitalists. At that point we have the capital–labour relation. If

the means of consumption belonged to workers themselves, it would be senseless for them to sell them and then buy them back, because they need them to reproduce their lives in the first place. In fact workers are required to buy and consume the means of life as commodities because those means of life are alienated from them.

3. Pre-capitalist economic formations are properly understood only from the standpoint of the circuit of money-capital, which represents the expansion of capital into the world market. This appears in Marx's *Grundrisse* manuscripts (N 459 line 8 – 515 line 40, M 367 line 34 – 417 line 21) as 'the expanded Forms', on which he grounds his materialist understanding of history and the contemporary world, as summarised in the Preface to *A contribution to the critique of political economy* of 1859.

4. *Manuscripts (1844)*, p. 364.

5. *Science of logic*, p. 405, quotation partially altered.

6. *Science of logic*, p. 406.

7. *Capital*, vol. 1, p. 269.

8. *Science of logic*, p. 395; quotation largely altered.

9. *Science of logic*, p. 398; quotation largely altered.

10. *Science of logic*, p. 433.

11. *Science of logic*, p. 435; quotation partially altered.

12. Cf. *Science of logic*, pp. 444 ff.; Hegel's *Logic*, sects 121 – 2.

13. Cf. Sekisuke Mita, *Studies of Hegel's Major Logic* (*Hegel Daironrigaku Kenkyu*) vol. 2 (Tokyo: Otsuki Shoten, 1980), pp. 212 – 22. Although this study is full of suggestions concerning the relation of the *Grundrisse* (or of *Capital*) to Hegel's *Logic*, many references are merely fragmentary and do not treat the relation systematically.

14. *Science of logic*, p. 455; quotation largely altered.

15. Cf. 'The two [content and matter] are distinguished from each other in that, though matter in itself is not without form, it manifests itself indifferently with respect to whatever form is in existence, whereas content is what it is, only in that it includes the developed form in itself' (Hegel's *Logic*, sect. 133, Z; quotation largely altered).

16. Cf. 'It [M – C – C – M] is the first movement in which exchange-value as such forms the content [*der Inhalt*] — is not only form [*Form*] but also its own content [*Gehalt*]' (N 253, M 176). On the different ways that Marx and Hegel understand 'form as content' see Michael Brie, 'Zur Dialektik von Inhalt und Form in den *Grundrissen der Kritik der politischen Ökonomie*', *Wissenschaftliche Zeitschrift der Homboldt-Universität zur Berlin*, XXXII (1983), p. 31.

In the first edition (1867) of *Capital*, vol. 1, Marx writes: 'It is scarcely surprising that economists have overlooked the form-content [*Forminhalt*] of the relative value-expression (subjected as they are to the influence of material interests), if professional logicians before *Hegel* even overlooked the content of form [*Formgehalt*] in the paradigms of judgements and syllogisms' ('The Commodity', in *Value – Studies by Marx*, p. 22).

17. Cf. 'Aristotle thought that everything concrete consists of two elements [ex amphoin]; i.e. form and matter. The case is the same with the human being. It consists of body and mind, the former he understands as form, the latter as matter. He tended to comprehend the two together, grasping matter or body as possibility, and form or mind as actuality'

(Kiyoshi Miki, 'Of metaphysics in the future' ('Keijijyogaku no Shorai nitsuite'), in *Collected works of Kiyoshi Miki* (*Miki Kiyoshi Zenshu*), vol. 5 (Tokyo: Iwanami Shoten, 1967), p. 43).

18. Cf. Gould, *Marx's social ontology*, pp. 45–6, where she confuses the labour-process with the valorisation process. However, Gould discusses the Marx–Aristotle relationship and makes many valuable suggestions in her book.

19. Cf. *Science of logic*, pp. 555 ff.

20. Cf. *Science of logic*, pp. 499 ff.

21. Cf. *Science of logic*, pp. 513 ff.

22. Cf. Marx's critique of Ricardo's pseudo-naturalism in the *Grundrisse* (N 331, M 246).

23. Marx had already considered the difficulties in section (3) 'Commodities as the Product of Capital' in *Results of the immediate process of production*, in *Capital*, vol. 1, pp. 949–75, where his manuscript *Results* are arranged as he wrote them. See also *Value — Studies by Marx*, pp. 159–82, where this material is edited according to Marx's intentions as revealed in the manuscripts.

In the original version of the *Results*, as it appears in the *Grundrisse*, Marx discusses firstly, the relation between relative surplus-value and profit, and secondly, the relation between the motive for investing in machinery and the results of such investment. These two points form 'the twofold problem of constant capital', which concerns the problem of the reproduction of capital through exchange (N 439–43, M 350–3).

This twofold problem has a profound effect on the rearrangement of the manuscripts of the *Grundrisse* to conform with the 'Draft plan of 1859' and on the interpretation of the order in which the manuscripts of the *Critique of political economy 1861–3* were written, especially Chapter 3 'Capital and Profit'. These manuscripts were in fact written before *Theories of surplus-value* and section (8) 'Machinery', contrary to the newly published version in *Marx–Engels Gesamtausgabe (MEGA)*. Cf. Hiroshi Uchida, 'The theoretical effective range of the twofold problem of constant capital' ('Nijyuno Fuhenshihon Mondai no Rironshatei'), *Economic Bulletin of Senshu University* (Tokyo), vol. 21 (1986).

24. *Science of logic*, pp. 518 ff.

25. *Manuscripts (1844)*, p. 324; quotation largely altered.

26. *Manuscripts (1844)*, p. 395; quotation largely altered.

27. *Manuscripts (1844)*, p. 386; quotation partially altered.

28. *Phenomenology of spirit*, p. 213; quotation partially altered. Hegel had already recognised the interdependence of individuals that arises through the exchange of products of labour, with reference to Smith's *Wealth of nations*, which he had perhaps read during his stay in Berne 1793–6. In his *First philosophy of spirit* (1803–4) he writes '. . . man no longer works up what he uses himself, or he uses no longer what he has worked up himself; that becomes only the possibility of his satisfaction instead of the actual satisfaction of his needs; his labour becomes a *formally abstract general*, a singular [factor]; he limits himself to labour for one of his needs, and exchanges it for whatever is necessary for his other needs. His labour is for *need* [in general], it is for the abstraction of a need as generally suffered, not for his need; and the satisfaction of the totality of his needs is a *labour of*

everyone. Between the range of needs of the single [agent], and his activity on their account, there enters the labour of the whole people, and the labour of any one is in respect of *its contents, a general labour of the needs of all*, so as to be *appropriate for the satisfaction of all of his needs*; in other words it has a *value* . . . need and labour are elevated into the form of consciousness; they are simplified, but their simplicity is formally general abstract simplicity . . . the *division of labour* increases *the mass* of manufactured [objects]; eighteen men work in an English pin factory [Smith, (*Wealth of nations* — HU, p. 8]' (Hegel, *First philosophy of spirit*, pp. 247–8; quotation partially altered).

29. Martin Nicolaus may be correct in his translation of the German *Versachlichung* as 'objectification' (N 160), if he is aware of its implications. However, he gives *sachliche Bedingungen* two translations: 'objective conditions' (N 453) and 'material conditions' (N 454), so it is not clear if he understands the implications fully.

30. Cf. 'When all the conditions of a matter of concern [*alle Bedingungen einer Sache*] are completely present, it enters into actuality; the completeness of the conditions is the totality as in the content, and *the matter of concern itself* [*die Sache selbst*] is this content determined as being as actual as possible' (*Science of logic*, p. 548; quotation partially altered).

31. *Science of logic*, pp. 551–2.

32. *Capital*, vol. 1, pp. 729–30.

33. Cf. 'But the self is only *abstractly* conceived man, man produced by abstraction. Man *is* selfish [*selbstlich*]. His eyes, his ears, etc., are *selfish*; each one of his essential powers has the property of *selfishness*. But therefore it is quite wrong to say that *self-consciousness* has eyes, ears, essential power' (*Manuscripts (1844)*, p. 387; quotation partially altered). Marx thinks that what Hegel calls 'self' is the consciousness of bourgeois ownership of things (*Sachen*), including one's own body. Cf. Uchida, 'The money of the spirit', p. 23. Following on from the *Economic and philosophical manuscripts (1844)* Marx writes in the *Grundrisse*: '[Man has *labour-power* as far as it is termed the capital of the labourer, as it is a fund, which he does not consume in an isolated exchange, but can always repeat anew during his life. Therefore all that is capital, that is, the fund for a repeated] process undergone by the same subject; so, e.g. the substance of the eye is the capital of seeing' (N 293, M 212; the text in square brackets is given only in *Marx–Engels Gesamtasugabe (MEGA)*, II/1.1, p. 212). Marx criticises the view that sight, which is given at birth, is taken for a determination of capital. This perverse misunderstanding had already been manifested in John Locke's theory that property is based on 'one's own labour'. Locke attributes the legitimacy of private property to its being a resultant of the labour or activity of one's own body, something which God gives impartially to each human being as property.

34. *Science of logic*, p. 567; quotation largely altered.

35. Cf. 'Therefore, though the cause has an effect *and is at the same time itself effect*, and the effect not only has a cause but *is also itself cause*, yet the effect which the cause *has*, and the effect *which the cause is*, are different, as are also the cause which the effect *has*, and the cause *which the effect is*' (*Science of logic*, pp. 565–6).

36. Professor Shiro Sugihara has established that the author of this

pamphlet is Charles Wentworth Dilke (1789–1864); see his *Economics and economists* (*Keizaigaku to Keizaigakusha*), (Tokyo: Nihonkeizaihyoronsha, 1985), pp. 55 ff. See also Sir Charles Wentworth Dilke (1843–1911, grandson of the author), *The paper of a critique*, vol. 1 (London: John Murray, 1875), pp. 14–15; and *Dictionary of national biography*, ed. L. Stephen, vol. XV (London: Smith, Elder & Co., 1888), p. 76.

37. Cf. *Phenomenology of spirit*, pp. 111 ff.

Chapter 4

1. N 549–618, M 446–505 constitute the section on previous theories of surplus-value (*Ur-Theorien*).

2. Cf. *Science of logic*, pp. 650 ff.

3. $M-C<A_a+P_m$ is the present author's notation.

4. Cf. *Science of logic*, pp. 652 ff.

5. *Science of logic*, p. 488; quotation partially altered.

6. Cf. 'The place where all capital, circulating as well as fixed, not only originally but continually comes from is the appropriation of alien labour. But this process presupposes, as we have seen, a continuous small-scale circulation, the exchange of wages for labour-power, or *approvisionnement* (N 734, M 609).

7. 'One capital' is one of the determinations of 'capital in general' in the *Grundrisse*; others are 'the totality of various determinations', 'the abstraction of concrete forms of capital', 'the total capital of a nation (capital of the whole society)', etc.

8. Cf. *Science of logic*, pp. 653 ff.

9. Hegel's 'ruse of reason', his method of grasping unexpected social results, might be said to resemble Smith's method. Smith distinguished efficient cause from final cause when he considered social and economic phenomena in *The theory of moral sentiments* and in *The wealth of nations*.

10. Marx's materialism can be described as follows: 'The doctrine, that *nature* signifies *creation* and *creature* at once, and furthermore that *nature* signifies *the creation of the creature*, is one of the traditional doctrines of Europe, which derives from ancient Greece. Everything is simultaneously a creature and is engaged in creation (history of nature); human beings are the essence of nature; the natural environment is humanized by human nature (creation), which itself is a result of creation (reciprocal determinations of the history of humankind and of nature). A good understanding of this doctrine is indispensable to the comprehension of "nature" or "human essence" in the *Economic and philosophical manuscripts (1844)*'; see Yoshihiko Uchida, *The concept of society in process* (*Shakaininshiki no Ayumi*) (Tokyo: Iwanami Shoten, 1971), pp. 83–4.

Chapter 5

1. Cf. *Science of logic*, pp. 629 f.

2. The extent to which Hegel's study of *The wealth of nations* was a formative influence on the *Science of logic* remains to be investigated. Book I

of *The wealth of nations* seems to correspond to the 'doctrine of being' in the *Science of logic*, and Book II to the 'doctrine of essence'.

3. *Science of logic*, p. 447; quotation partially altered.

4. *Science of logic*, p. 447; quotation partially altered.

5. Marx's conception of capital as 'a determinate totality' or 'one capital' with complex determinations is related to Hegel's definition of syllogism as 'one' formed through a mediating circulation.

6. *Capital*, vol. 1, p. 734.

7. Luxury is contained within the capitalist's means of consumption as a symbol of class. The social reproduction of capital, including capitalist luxuries, requires change from 'one capital' to 'many capitals', which is one of the points of transition from the *Grundrisse* to the *Critique of political economy 1861–3*. In the *Grundrisse* 'one capital' represents the whole of capitalist society, but when analysed in the process of reproduction, it represents one industrial sector. Cf. Marx's analysis of the exchange between 'capital a' and 'capital b' (N 730–1, M 606).

8. Marx's first attempt at describing primitive accumulation was in *The German ideology*, cf. Karl Marx and Friedrich Engels, *Die deutsche Ideologie*, Part One, Volume One, ed. W. Hiromatsu (Tokyo: Kawade-shoboshinsha, 1974), pp. 90–112. This edition is based on a critical reassessment of the principal German editions, including that of V. V. Adoratskij, which Professor Hiromatsu condemns as 'a *de facto* forgery'. Use of Hiromatsu's edition is indispensable for further study of *The German ideology*.

9. Those transformations are accompanied by the subsumption of immediate producers under capital. In the *Grundrisse* the following two sorts of subsumption are defined as 'formal': (a) subsumption of small-scale producers (weavers and spinners) under commercial capital, which puts out cloth and yarn through commodity exchange with producers, and (b) subsumption of wage-labourers under manufacturing capital. The subsumption of wage-labourers under the system of machine-production is defined as 'real'. In Marx's *Critique of political economy 1861–3* the connection between the seemingly independent producers and commercial capital through a relation of sale and purchase is excluded from 'formal subsumption'. That alteration occurs as a result of Marx's conversion from grasping 'one capital', which he does from the viewpoint of the circuit of money-capital in the *Grundrisse* (cf. N 586–7, M 477–8; N 853–4, 858–9, M 716–17, 721) to developing 'many capitals'. In the *Critique of political economy 1861–3* he does this from the standpoint of the circuit of commodity-capital.

10. Cf. 'The *immediate idea* is *life*. As *soul*, the notion is realized in a body, of whose externality [*von dessen Äusserlichkeit*] . . .' (Hegel's *Logic*, sect. 216).

11. Cf. Wataru Hiromatsu, *The composition of the theory of reification* (*Versachlichung*) (*Busshokaron no Kozu*), (Tokyo: Iwanami Shoten, 1983), pp. 125 ff.

12. Professor Kiyoaki Hirata correctly interprets Marx's comment on settling 'accounts [*abzurechnen*] with our former philosophical conscience [*Gewissen*]' (from the Preface to *A contribution to the critique of political economy* of 1859), when he writes that it does not mean annulling philosophical

consciousness, but squaring accounts of philosophical *conscience*, balancing credits and debits. Cf. K. Hirata (ed.), *The history of social thought* (*Shakaishisoshi*) (Tokyo: Seirinshoin Shinsha, 1979), p. 342. If the German *abzurechnen* signifies 'annulling', why does Marx continue to study Hegel's works, including the *Logic*, after 1859?

Select Bibliography

Aristotle

The complete works of Aristotle, ed. J. Barnes, 2 vols, Princeton University Press, Princeton NJ (1984)

G. W. F. Hegel

Enzyklopädie der philosophischen Wissenschaften, vol. 1, Suhrkamp Verlag, Frankfurt (1970)

Hegel's logic, trans. W. Wallace, Oxford University Press, Oxford (1975)

Jenaer Systementwürfe, I, *Gesammelte Werke*, vol. 6, Felix Meiner Verlag, Hamburg (1975)

Phänomenologie des Geistes, Suhrkamp Verlag, Frankfurt (1970)

Phenomenology of spirit, trans. A. V. Miller, Oxford University Press, Oxford (1977)

Philosophy of right, trans. T. M. Knox, Clarendon Press, Oxford (1965)

Science of logic, trans. A. V. Miller, George Allen & Unwin, London (1969)

Science of logic, trans. W. H. Johnston and L. G. Struthers, 2 vols, George Allen & Unwin, London (1929)

System of ethical life (1802/3) and First philosophy of spirit, trans. and ed. H. S. Harris and T. M. Knox, State University of New York Press, Albany NY (1979)

Wissenschaft der Logik, I–II, Suhrkamp Verlag, Frankfurt (1969)

Karl Marx

Capital, vol. 1, trans. Ben Fowkes; vol. 2, trans. David Fernbach; vol. 3, trans. David Fernbach, Penguin Books, Harmondsworth (1976–8)

Economic and philosophical manuscripts (1844), trans. Gregor Benton in *Early writings*, Penguin Books, Harmondsworth (1975)

Grundrisse: foundations of the critique of political economy (rough draft), trans. Martin Nicolaus, Penguin Books, Harmondworth (1973)

Marx's Grundrisse, trans. and ed. David McLellan, Macmillan, London (1971)

'Marx's précis of Hegel's doctrine of being in the Minor Logic', ed. F. E. Schrader, intro. J. O'Malley, *International Review of Social History*, vol. XXII (1977), pp. 423–31

Marx–Engels Werke, vols 29–31, Dietz Verlag, East Berlin (1963–5)

Die Ökonomisch-philosophische Manuskripte, Marx–Engels Gesamtausgabe (MEGA), I/2, Dietz Verlag, East Berlin (1982)

Ökonomische Manuskripte 1857/58, 1–2, *Marx–Engels Gesamtausgabe (MEGA)*, II/1.1, 1.2, Dietz Verlag, East Berlin (1976, 1981)

Resultate des unmittelbaren produktionsprozesses, Verlag Neue Kritik, Frankfurt (1969)
Value: studies by Karl Marx, New Park Publications, London (1976)
Über 'Das Kapital': Briefwechsel, Dietz Verlag, East Berlin (1985)

Adam Smith

An inquiry into the nature and causes of the wealth of nations, ed. E. Cannan, Methuen, London (1950)

Other works

Albritton, R. (1986) *A Japanese reconstruction of Marxist theory*, Macmillan, London
Arthur, C. J. (1986) *Dialectics of labour: Marx and his relation to Hegel*, Basil Blackwell, Oxford
Bernd, F. (1979) 'Zur Entwicklung der Auffassungen von Karl Marx über fixes und zirkulierendes Kapital von 1857 bis 1863' in *Marx–Engels–Jahrbuch*, 1, Dietz Verlag, East Berlin
Carver, T. (1975) *Karl Marx: texts on method*, Basil Blackwell, Oxford
Carver, T. (1976) 'Marx — and Hegel's *Logic*', *Political Studies*, vol. XXIV, pp. 57–68
Carver, T. (1982) *Marx's social theory*, Oxford University Press, Oxford
Carver, T. (1983) *Marx and Engels: the intellectual relationship*, Wheatsheaf Books, Brighton
Colletti, L. (1973) *Marxism and Hegel*, trans. L. Garner, New Left Books, London
Cullen, B. (1979) *Hegel's social and political thought: an introduction*, Gill and Macmillan, London
Echeverria, R. (1978) 'Critique of Marx's 1857 introduction', *Economy and Society*, vol. 7, pp. 333–66
Fenves, P. (1986) 'Marx's doctoral thesis on two Greek atomists and the post-Kantian interpretations', *Journal of the History of Ideas*, vol. XLVII, pp. 433–52
Fo, M. (1973) *The essence of Hegel's dialectics* (*Hegel Benshoho no Honshitusu*), Aokishoten, Tokyo
Gould, C. C. (1978) *Marx's social ontology: individuality and community in Marx's theory of social reality*, MIT Press, Cambridge MA
Harris, H. S. (1972) *Hegel's development: towards the sunlight (1770–1801)*, Oxford University Press, Oxford
Harris, H. S. (1983) *Hegel's development: night thoughts (Jena 1801–1806)*, Oxford University Press, Oxford
Hirata, K. (1972) *Political economy and the recognition of history* (*Keizaigaku to Rekishininshiki*), Iwanami Shoten, Tokyo
Hirata, K. (1982) *A methodological introduction to the critique of political economy* (*Keizaigakuhihan eno Hohojyosetsu*), Iwanami Shoten, Tokyo
Hiromatsu, W. (1980) *The logic of dialectics* (*Benshoho no Ronri*), Seidosha, Tokyo

Hiromatsu, W. (ed.) (1986) *Reading 'Capital' from the viewpoint of reification (Versachlichung) (Shihonron o Busshokaron o Shijiku ni shite Yomu)*, Iwanami Shoten, Tokyo

Hook, S. (1936) *From Hegel to Marx: studies in the intellectual development of Karl Marx*, Reynal & Hitchcock, New York

Hosomi, H. (1979) *Critique of political economy and dialectics (Keizaigakuhihan to Benshoho)*, Miraisha, Tokyo

Kakehashi, A. (1959) *Hegel's philosophy and Capital (Hegel Tetsugaku to Shihonron)*, Miraisha, Tokyo

Krahl, H.-J. (1970) 'Bemerkungen zum Verhältnis von Kapital und Hegelscher Wesenlogik' in *Aktualität und Folgen der Philosophie Hegels*, ed. O. von Negt, Suhrkamp Verlag, Frankfurt

Krämer-Badomi, T. (1978) *Zur Legitimität der bürgerlichen Gesellschaft*, Campul Verlag, Frankfurt

Labica, G. and Delbraccio, M. (1985) *Étudier Marx*, Éditions du Centre National de le Recherche Scientifique, Paris

Lukács, G. (1975) *The young Hegel: studies in the relations between dialectics and economics*, trans. R. Livingstone, Merlin Press, London

McBride, W. L. (1977) *The philosophy of Marx*, Hutchinson, London

McTaggart, J. (1931) *A commentary on Hegel's Logic*, Cambridge University Press, Cambridge

Marquit, E. (1977–8) 'Nicolaus and Marx's method of scientific theory in the *Grundrisse*', *Science and Society*, vol. 41, 465–76

Martin-Luther-Universität (1976–86) *Arbeitsblätter zur Marx-Engels-Forschung*, 1–20

Meikle, S. (1985) *Essentialism in the thought of Karl Marx*, Duckworth, London

Mepham, J. (1979) 'From the *Grundrisse* to *Capital*: the making of Marx's method' in *Issues in Marxist philosophy*, vol. 1, *Dialectics and method*, ed. J. Mepham and D.-H. Ruben, Harvester Press, Brighton

Mercier-Josa, S. (1986) *Retour sur le jeune Marx: Deux études sur le rapport de Marx à Hegel*, Méridiens, Paris

Mita, S. (1963) *The method of Capital (Shihonron no Hoho)*, Kobundo, Tokyo

Mochizuki, S. (1974) *A study of Marx's theory of history (Marx Rekishiriron no Kenkyu)*, Iwanami Shoten, Tokyo

Mure, G. R.G. (1950) *A study of Hegel's Logic*, Oxford University Press, Oxford

Neumann, W. (1982) *Der unbewusste Hegel: Zum Verhältnis der Wissenschaft der Logik zu Marx' Kritik der politischen Ökonomie*, Materialis Verlag, Frankfurt

Niji, Y. (1978) *A study of value-form (Kachikeitairon)*, Aokishoten, Tokyo

O'Malley, J., K. W. Algozin, H. P. Kainz, and L. C. Rice (eds) (1973) *The legacy of Hegel*, Martinus Nijhoff, The Hague

O'Malley, J. (1976) 'Marx's "Economics" and Hegel's *Philosophy of right*: an essay on Marx's Hegelianism', *Political Studies*, vol. XXIV, pp. 43–56

Otsuka, H. (1982) *The spirit of capitalism: the Max Weber thesis in an economic historical perspective*, trans. M. Kondo, Iwanami Shoten, Tokyo

Patrick, S. (1974) 'Aristotle's concept of matter and its relation to modern concepts of matter', *Synthese*, vol. 28, pp. 27–50

Pelczynski, Z. A. (ed.) (1984) *The state and civil society: studies in Hegel's political philosophy*, Cambridge University Press, Cambridge.

Rojek, C. (1985) *Capitalism and leisure theory*, Tavistock Publications, London

Rosdolsky, R. (1977) *The making of Marx's 'Capital'*, trans. P. Burgess, Pluto Press, London

Rotenstreich, N. (1974) *From substance to subject*, Martinus Nijhoff, The Hague

Saegusa, H. (1931) *The dialectics of Capital* (*Shihonron no Benshoho*), Jichosha, Tokyo

Schmidt, A. (1971) *The concept of nature in Marx*, trans. B. Fowkes, New Left Books, London

Schnädelbach, H. (1984) *Philosophy in Germany 1831–1933*, trans. E. Matthews, Cambridge University Press, Cambridge

Schrader, F. E. (1980) *Restauration und Revolution: Die Vorarbeiten zum 'Kapital' von Karl Marx in seinen Studienheften 1850–1858*, Gerstenberg Verlag, Hildesheim

Schwarz, W. (1978) *Von 'Rohentwurf' zum 'Kapital': Die Strukturgeschichte dès Marxschen Hauptwerkes*, Verlag das Europäische Buch, West Berlin

Sekine, T. (1984) *Dialectic of Capital*, vol. 1, Yushindo Press, Tokyo

Spicer, E. E. (1934) *Aristotle's conception of the soul*, University of London Press, London

Sugihara, S. (1957) *J. S. Mill and Marx (Mill to Marx)*, Minerva Shobo, Kyoto

Sugihara, S. (1973) *Principles of political economy* (*Keizaigenron*), vol. 1, Dobunkan, Tokyo

Takechi, T. (1947–8) *The world of Hegel's Science of logic* (*Hegel Ronrigaku no Sekai*), Hukumurashuppan, Tokyo

Uchida, H. (1982) *A study of the Grundrisse* (*Keizaigakuhihanyoko no Kenkyu*), Shinhyoron, Tokyo

Uchida, H. (1985) *Marx's middle-period critique of political economy* (*Chuki Marx no Keizaigakuhihan*), Yuhikaku, Tokyo

Uchida, H. (1986) 'The money of the spirit: the young Marx's analysis of the homology between political economy and Hegel's philosophy', *Monthly Report of the Institute for Social Sciences of Senshu University* (Tokyo), 272, pp. 2–30; 20 March; published in English

della Volpe, G. (1980) *Logic as a positive science*, trans. J. Rothschild, New Left Books, London

Winfield, R. (1976) 'The logic of Marx's Capital', *Telos*, 27, pp. 111–39

Yamada, T. (1985) *The vision of modern civil society in Marx's Critique of political economy* (*Keizaigakuhihan no Kindaizo*), Yuhikaku, Tokyo

Zelený, J. (1980) *The logic of Marx*, trans. T. Carver, Basil Blackwell, Oxford

Index

For Product Safety Concerns and Information please contact our EU representative GPSR@taylorandfrancis.com
Taylor & Francis Verlag GmbH, Kaufingerstraße 24, 80331 München, Germany

www.ingramcontent.com/pod-product-compliance
Lightning Source LLC
LaVergne TN
LVHW021039011026
849160LV00008BA/642

* 9 7 8 1 1 3 8 8 8 8 5 3 1 *

TABLE OF CONTENTS

CHAPTER 1

A Timely Play

Malcolm Butler stands in the **end zone**. He looks at the Seattle Seahawks offense. He eyes a **wide receiver**. Russell Wilson is Seattle's quarterback. He calls out a play. Butler's New England Patriots are in a tough spot. Seattle needs just one more yard to score.

It is the Super Bowl. New England leads 28–24. Only 27 seconds remain. Seattle could score. Then the Seahawks would probably win.

Wilson gets the ball. He quickly turns his body to his right. He throws the ball. It goes toward Ricardo Lockette.

FUN FACT

The 2014 Seahawks allowed the fewest points in the league.

New England linebacker Rob Ninkovich (50) sacks Seattle quarterback Russell Wilson in Super Bowl XLIX.

Malcom Butler makes the game-winning interception in Super Bowl XLIX.

Butler is right next to Lockette. He doesn't want the receiver to catch the ball. It could mean a touchdown. The ball comes their way. Butler gets in front of Lockette. He grabs the ball. **Interception**!

Butler's teammates start to celebrate. Butler runs forward. He drops to the ground. The Patriots players hug. They throw their hands in the air. They cannot believe what Butler just did. Wilson walks off the field. He looks at the ground. He was sad at how the game ended. The Patriots won 28–24. They were Super Bowl champions!

LEGION OF BOOM

Richard Sherman stands next to a wide receiver. Earl Thomas is behind him. Kam Chancellor stands to his left. Malcolm Smith is closer to the quarterback. These were all Seattle Seahawks defensive players. They were some of the NFL's best. They were known as the Legion of Boom. They helped Seattle make it to multiple Super Bowls in the 2010s.

Football fans love offense. But defense is also important. These players work together to stop the offense. A good defense can change a game. There have been many great defenses in National Football League (NFL) history.

Malcolm Butler (21) celebrates with teammate Julian Edelman after winning the Super Bowl.

Patriots
NFL
SUPER BOWL
XLIX

12
Patriots

CHAPTER 2

Working Together

The Chicago Bears defense runs onto the field. There are eleven players. They have to work together. Only they can stop the other team's offense.

The 2018 Bears defense was one of the best in the league. It started with the two defensive tackles. They play right next to the ball. Akiem Hicks is on one side. He is a big player. His size makes him tough to block. He runs straight ahead. He has a simple job. He has to stop the player with the ball. He cannot let the player get by.

FUN FACT

The Chicago Bears are known for great linebackers. They have five in the Pro Football Hall of Fame.

Akiem Hicks bears down on Minnesota Vikings quarterback Kirk Cousins in 2018.

Khalil Mack stands to the right of Hicks. He is ready to take off. The ball is **snapped**. Mack **sprints** past the offensive lineman. He sees the quarterback. Slam! Mack throws him to the ground. Players like Mack have to be fast. They can stop the offense quickly.

Roquan Smith stands behind Hicks. He's listening to what the coach says. The coach tells him how the defense should line up. Smith yells out to his teammates. Then the ball is snapped. Smith watches where the ball goes. Smith is a linebacker. These players lead the defense. They call out plays and do many other things.

An outside linebacker, Khalil Mack often plays on the line to rush the passer.

WHERE DEFENSIVE PLAYERS LINE UP

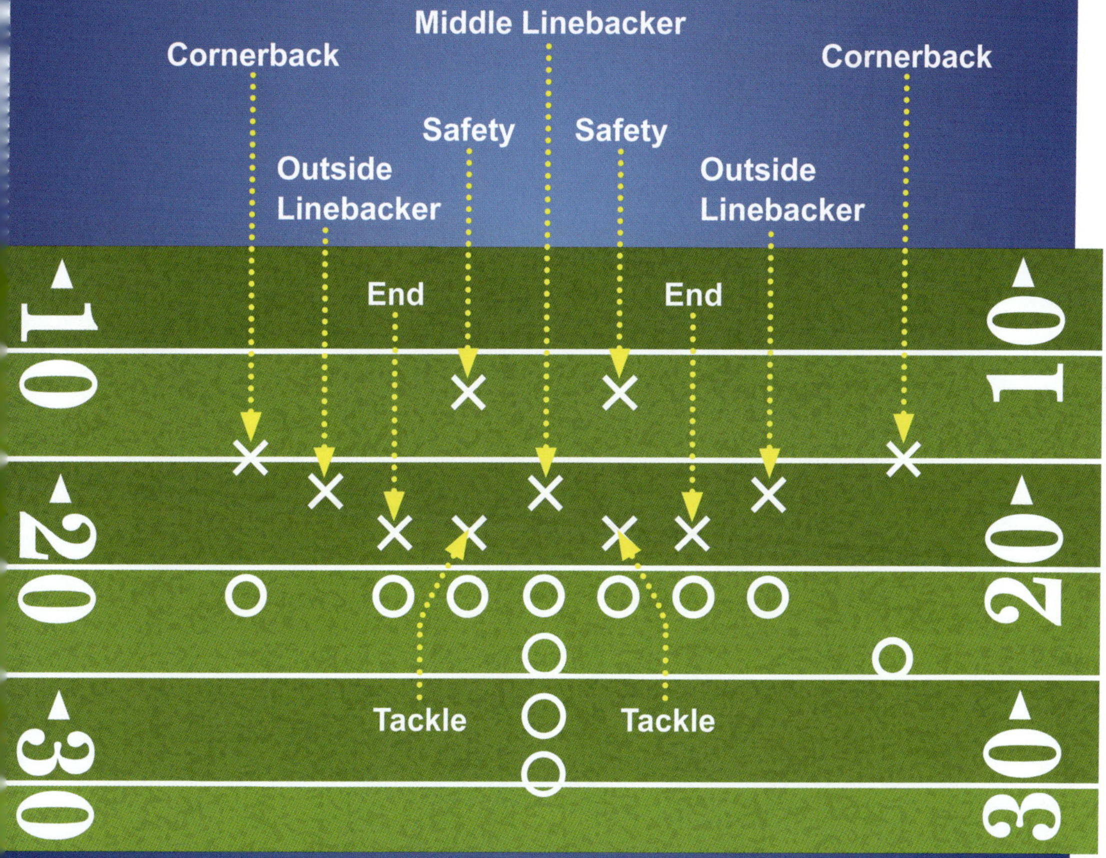

Eddie Jackson led the NFL with two interceptions returned for touchdowns in 2018.

Two players stand near the wide receivers. The ball is snapped. These players start running backward. They run with the receivers. They are the cornerbacks. Their job is to cover the receivers. Chicago had two good cornerbacks in Prince Amukamara and Kyle Fuller.

Two players stand in the center of the field. They are farthest away from the quarterback. These are safeties. They move farther back when the play starts. They are watching the ball. It is thrown to a receiver. Safety Eddie Jackson runs to the ball. He grabs it out of the air. Good safeties help slow down receivers. Players like Jackson are good at forcing **turnovers**.

CHAPTER 3

Lawrence Taylor was named NFL Defensive Player of the Year three times in his thirteen-year career.

All Sizes

Lawrence Taylor starts running at the quarterback. He chases him down. He slams him to the ground. Taylor was one of the greatest players of all time. He starred for the New York Giants. His best years came in the 1980s. Many consider Taylor to be the best defensive player in NFL history.

Fast forward to a few years later. Fans watched Reggie White play. He was bigger than Taylor. But he still got around linemen with no problem. He won a Super Bowl with the Green Bay Packers. Packers fans loved White. They cheered wildly when he **sacked** the quarterback.

NICKNAMES

Defenses have received many nicknames. Alan Page and Jim Marshall lined up for the Minnesota Vikings. They were part of a group called the Purple People Eaters. "Mean" Joe Greene was a star for the Pittsburgh Steelers. He was part of the Steel Curtain. Mike Singletary lined up for the Chicago Bears in the 1980s. He was one of the Monsters of the Midway.

Deion Sanders was an incredible athlete. He also played Major League Baseball.

It is the 1990s. Deion Sanders stands in his black Atlanta Falcons jersey. He is very close to a wide receiver. The ball is snapped. Sanders runs with the receiver. There is little room between the two. The quarterback throws to the receiver anyway.

The ball floats in the air. Sanders jumps up. Interception! Sanders starts running the other way. Sanders was one of the best defensive backs in the NFL. Teams were afraid to throw the ball near him.

TIMELINE OF TOP DEFENSIVE PLAYERS

1965

Dick Butkus, linebacker: Chicago Bears *(1965–73)*

"Mean" Joe Greene, defensive tackle: Pittsburgh Steelers *(1969–81)*

1975

Lawrence Taylor, linebacker: New York Giants *(1981–93)*

1985

Reggie White, defensive lineman: Philadelphia Eagles *(1985–92)*, Green Bay Packers *(1993–98)*, Carolina Panthers *(2000)*

Deion Sanders, cornerback: Atlanta Falcons *(1989–93)*, San Francisco 49ers *(1994)*, Dallas Cowboys *(1995–99)*, Washington Redskins *(2000)*, Baltimore Ravens *(2004–05)*

1995

Ed Reed, safety: Baltimore Ravens *(2002–12)*, New York Jets *(2013)*, Houston Texans *(2013)*

2005

J.J. Watt, defensive end: Houston Texans *(2011–)*

2015

Khalil Mack, linebacker: Oakland Raiders *(2014–17)*, Chicago Bears *(2018–)*

Troy Polamalu stands in the center of the field. His long hair bounces off his back. He sees the ball snapped. He looks around at the developing play. A wide receiver is running in the middle of the field. Polamalu gets close to him. The ball is thrown toward the receiver.

Polamalu launches himself. Boom! Polamalu runs into the wide receiver. The ball falls to the ground. Polamalu was one of the best defensive backs in NFL history. Pittsburgh Steelers fans loved watching him play in the 2000s.

FUN FACT

Polamalu was one of many NFL players of American Samoan descent.

Troy Polamalu was known for his long hair and his big hits.

CHAPTER 4

Aaron Donald led the NFL in sacks in 2018 with 20.5.

Today's Speedsters

Aaron Donald comes flying up the middle. He throws down the quarterback. Donald is one of the best defensive tackles in the league. He plays for the Los Angeles Rams. Donald is big and strong. But he is also fast. He runs quickly to the ball. Teams run away from Donald. He was named the NFL's Defensive Player of the Year in 2018. It was the second time he won that award.

Bobby Wagner stands near the ball. The ball is snapped. Wagner sprints toward the quarterback. He gets by one blocker. He runs straight into the quarterback. It's a sack!

The ball hits the ground. Wagner sees it. He jumps on it. Wagner is one of the NFL's best linebackers. He causes problems for offenses. He leads the Seattle Seahawks defense.

The quarterback throws a pass high in the air. He's looking for a receiver down the field. But he's covered by two players. One of those is Harrison Smith of the Minnesota Vikings. He leaps in the air. He grabs the ball with two hands. Interception! Safeties like Smith are hard to find. He's quick and can make game-changing plays.

FUN FACT

There are two types of safety: free safety and strong safety.

BOBBY WAGNER

CAREER STATS

Through the 2018 season

GAMES PLAYED	103
SACKS	16.5
TACKLES	591
TOUCHDOWNS	4
FORCED FUMBLES	4

Denzel Ward (21) blocks a field goal attempt in a 2018 game.

Denzel Ward of the Cleveland Browns runs backward. He is right next to the receiver. The receiver wants the ball. But the quarterback throws it to another player. The quarterback is afraid of Ward. Ward is one of the most exciting young defensive backs in the league.

Defense can play a role in every game. Players continue to get faster. They are also stronger. They will keep making it tough for offenses to score. Fans are excited to see the next great group of defenders.

BEYOND THE BOOK

After reading the book, it's time to think about what you learned. Try the following exercises to jumpstart your ideas.

THINK

DIFFERENT SOURCES. Think about what types of sources you could find on the 2018 Chicago Bears defense. What could you find in a news article? What could you learn from the Bears website? What about an interview with a sports writer? How could each of the sources be useful in its own way?

CREATE

SHARPEN YOUR RESEARCH SKILLS. This book talks about great defensive players like Reggie White. Where could you go in the library to find more information about White? Who could you talk to who might know more? Create a research plan. Write a paragraph about your next steps.

SHARE

WHAT'S YOUR OPINION? In Chapter Two, it says that a defense is good when the entire group works together. Do you agree or disagree with this opinion? Use evidence from the text to support your answer. Share your position and evidence with a friend. Does your friend agree with you?

GROW

REAL-LIFE RESEARCH. What places could you visit to learn more about defensive backs? What other things could you learn while you were there?

RESEARCH NINJA

Visit www.ninjaresearcher.com/0745 to learn how to take your research skills and book report writing to the next level!

RESEARCH

DIGITAL LITERACY TOOLS

SEARCH LIKE A PRO
Learn about how to use search engines to find useful websites.

FACT OR FAKE?
Discover how you can tell a trusted website from an untrustworthy resource.

TEXT DETECTIVE
Explore how to zero in on the information you need most.

SHOW YOUR WORK
Research responsibly—learn how to cite sources.

WRITE

GET TO THE POINT
Learn how to express your main ideas.

PLAN OF ATTACK
Learn prewriting exercises and create an outline.

DOWNLOADABLE REPORT FORMS

Further Resources

BOOKS

Adamson, Thomas K. *The Seattle Seahawks Story.* Bellwether, 2017.

Challen, Paul C. *What Does a Defensive Back Do?* PowerKids Press, 2015.

Doeden, Matt. *Football's Greatest Defenders.* Capstone Press, 2015.

WEBSITES

FACTSURFER

Factsurfer.com gives you a safe, fun way to find more information.

1. Go to www.factsurfer.com.
2. Enter "Defensive Players" into the search box and click 🔍.
3. Select your book cover to see a list of related websites.

Glossary

end zone: The end zone is where someone has to go to score a touchdown. Bobby Wagner gets the ball and runs it into the end zone for a touchdown.

interception: An interception is when the defense catches a pass from the quarterback. Deion Sanders grabbed many interceptions in his career.

sacked: The quarterback is sacked when he is tackled for a loss of yardage. Aaron Donald sacked Tom Brady for a 10-yard loss.

snapped: When the center pitches the ball back to start a play, he has snapped it. Akiem Hicks took off for the quarterback after the ball was snapped.

sprints: To sprint means to run very quickly. Khalil Mack sprints to get to the quarterback.

turnovers: Turnovers occur when one team loses possession of the ball to the other team. The Chicago Bears defense led the NFL in turnovers in 2018.

wide receiver: An offensive football player who receives passes is called a wide receiver. Malcolm Butler intercepted a ball meant for the wide receiver.

Index

PHOTO CREDITS

The images in this book are reproduced through the courtesy of: Daniel Gluskoster/AP Images, front cover (left); Michael McGinnis/AP Images, front cover (center), p. 3; Greg Trott/AP Images, front cover (right); EFKS/Shutterstock Images, front cover (background); dean bertoncelj/Shutterstock Images, pp. 4, 19 (football), 24; Ben Liebenberg/AP Images, p. 5; Kathy Williens/AP Images, pp. 6–7; Perry Knotts/AP Images, pp. 8–9; Joseph Sohm/Shutterstock Images, p. 9; David Banks/AP Images, pp. 10–11, 14–15; Ryan Kang/AP Images, p. 12; Red Line Editorial, pp. 13, 19 (timeline), 25 (chart); Richard Cavalleri/Shutterstock Images, p. 15; Kathy Kmonicek/AP Images, p. 16; Al Messerschmidt/AP Images, p. 18; Gene J. Puskar/AP Images, pp. 20–21; Hiro Ueno/Los Angeles Rams/AP Images, pp. 22–23; Paul Abell/AP Images, p. 25 (Bobby Wagner); David Richard/AP Images, pp. 26–27; Olga Bogatyrenko/Shutterstock Images, p. 27; zieusin/Shutterstock Images, p. 30.

ABOUT THE AUTHOR

Kevin Frederickson is a freelance writer and editor from Ohio. He lives near Cincinnati with his golden doodle, Max.